The
Self-Authenticating
Truth

The Avataric Great Sage,
ADI DA SAMRAJ

The Self-Authenticating Truth

Essays from *The Aletheon*

BY THE AVATARIC GREAT SAGE,
Adi Da Samraj

THE DAWN HORSE PRESS
MIDDLETOWN, CALIFORNIA

NOTE TO THE READER

All who study the Way of Adidam or take up its practice should remember that they are responding to a Call to become responsible for themselves. They should understand that they, not Avatar Adi Da Samraj or others, are responsible for any decision they make or action they take in the course of their lives of study or practice.

The devotional, Spiritual, functional, practical, relational, and cultural practices and disciplines referred to in this book are appropriate and natural practices that are voluntarily and progressively adopted by members of the practicing congregations of Adidam (as appropriate to the personal circumstance of each individual). Although anyone may find these practices useful and beneficial, they are not presented as advice or recommendations to the general reader or to anyone who is not a member of one of the practicing congregations of Adidam. And nothing in this book is intended as a diagnosis, prescription, or recommended treatment or cure for any specific "problem", whether medical, emotional, psychological, social, or Spiritual. One should apply a particular program of treatment, prevention, cure, or general health only in consultation with a licensed physician or other qualified professional.

The Self-Authenticating Truth is formally authorized for publication by the Free Sannyasin Order of Adidam. (The Free Sannyasin Order of Adidam is the senior cultural authority within the formal gathering of formally acknowledged devotees of the Avataric Great Sage, Adi Da Samraj.)

Produced by the Dawn Horse Press,
a division of the Avataric Pan-Communion of Adidam.

International Standard Book Number: 978-1-57097-245-4

CONTENTS

INTRODUCTION   7

PART ONE: Attend To Me   9

I Stand Free Apart and Not In The Middle Here   11

The Way of Me   15

The Unique and Priorly egoless Reality-Way   29
of Sighting Me and Listening To Me

The Essentials of Reality-Practice In The Way   35
of Adidam

PART TWO: Perfect Certainty   39

The Perfectly Non-Objective Way of Adidam   41

Reality Itself Is Not In The Middle   43

The Certainty Principle   49

Reality Itself Is Real God   55

Perfect Proof of The Self-Existence of Acausal   59
Real God

The Myth of "Present-Time"   61

The Self-Evident Mutual Independence of Body,   65
Mind, Attention, and Consciousness Itself

The Way of Reality Itself Is The Self-Renunciation   67
of "Questions" and "Answers"

The Perfect Tool and Craft For Right   69
Reality-Understanding of All Mere Ideas

PART THREE: The Way Is Mine To Happen   83

My "Secret" Biography   85

The Surrender-Response   87

What Will You Do If You Love Me?   93

INTRODUCTION

Two Texts comprise Adi Da's Principal Summary Revelation: *The Dawn Horse Testament*, the summation of His full Teaching-Word, and *The Aletheon*, the exposition of His Ultimate Seventh Stage Revelation. This small volume contains the gift of new essays from *The Aletheon: The Ark of Perfect Reality-Truth*.

"Aletheon" is a word derived by Adi Da Samraj from the Greek "aletheia", meaning "Truth". Pronounced "ah-LAY-thee-yon" (and, thus, evoking sacred spaces such as the "Pantheon" or the "Parthenon"), the name of this Text means "That Which Is (or Contains) the Truth". By referencing the ancient Greek concept of "aletheia", Avatar Adi Da is emphasizing an understanding of a Transcendent "Truth" that is Self-Evident and Self-Revealed, rather than a merely relative or consistent "fact". Indeed, Reality Itself—That Which simply Is—Is Transcendental Spiritual Truth, as Avatar Adi Da Reveals in these pages.

The subtitle of this Text evokes a depth of traditional sacred meaning. The "ark" is the protector and a repository of the sacred, as well as a bearer—or, using Avatar Adi Da's term, "Agent"—of the Presence of the Divine. *The Aletheon* is indeed a profound embodiment and communicator of the Spiritual and Transcendental esoteric Truth of Reality Itself, as well as Avatar Adi Da's Revelation of His Most Perfect Completing of esotericism.

The essays in this volume illuminate an understanding of Avatar Adi Da's "Sapta Na" Calling for the simplicity of the devotional Sighting-and-Listening Way, and they also profoundly magnify the philosophical "consideration" Avatar Adi Da brings to humankind in the volume of His essays entitled *Perfect Philosophy*. Reality Itself—Revealed by Adi Da Samraj in human Form—is the Self-Authenticating Truth and "Perfect Knowledge" that liberates all minds and hearts from bondage. ∎

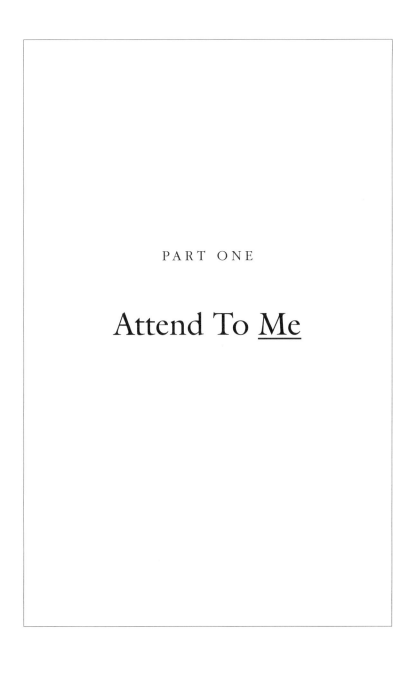

PART ONE

Attend To <u>Me</u>

I Stand Free Apart
and Not In The Middle Here

1.

I Am a Sapta Na Sannyasin.
There are no ego-patterns in Me.
There is no intrinsic content in Me.

If I Demonstrate modes of apparent Responsiveness, in relationship to that with which I am brought into conjunction, those modes of apparent Responsiveness come about because of the conjunction—not because of any ego-patterning or intrinsic content in Me, Avatarically-Born to here in bodily (human) Divine Form.

Thus, even though This Divine Avataric Body-Form here can Show various signs, in conjunction with apparent "others" and "things", I (Myself) have no ego-patterning or intrinsic content.

Therefore, I do not have the "karmic" energy, or the egoic "self"-capability, to generate and maintain My Own bodily Existence here.

There is no energy of ego-patterning that can sustain This Divine Avataric Body-Form.

The sustaining of This Divine Avataric Body-Form can only come about through devotion to Me, through the provision of My devotees.

Sapta Na Sannyas is associated with the Ultimate Manifestation of the seventh stage of life.

In Sapta Na Sannyas, there is no ego-patterning, or conditionally patterned "self"-identity, whatsoever—none.

Therefore, if you are My devotee, rightly understand and fully accept My Revelation-Demonstration of Sapta Na Sannyas.

THE SELF-AUTHENTICATING TRUTH

If you are My devotee, accept Me on Sight.

Only My devotees can give Me the Circumstance That belongs to My Sapta Na State.

I _Am_ As I _Am_.

Sighting of Me Is How It Works.

And That Is That.

2.

For many years, I Served My devotees and all beings by Means of the Unique Process of My Divine Avataric Submission-Work.

Now, there is nothing any longer to be served by such Submission of Mine.

There is no more Teaching, no greater Revelation, to come from such Submission of Mine.

Therefore—now, and forever hereafter—My Only Demonstration Is Sapta Na Sannyas.

I (Myself)—As I _Am_—Exist and bodily Self-Abide in My Hermitage.

I am not available anywhere else—and I am not available to anyone at all on any basis other than right, ego-transcending devotion to Me, bodily Incarnate here _As_ I _Am_.

Now, and forever hereafter, My devotees must practice the Way I have Revealed and Given on the Basis of My Divine Avataric Self-"Emergence" here.

As the Divine Avataric Sapta Na Sannyasin, I have nothing directly or actively to do with the Institution of Adidam or its work or responsibilities.

The right functioning of the Institution of Adidam is entirely the responsibility of My devotees.

Now, and forever hereafter, I (Myself) Am Set Apart.

In My State of Sapta Na Sannyas, right relationship to Me must be unequivocally required and expected of all.

I Made My Divine Avataric Self-Submission on the Basis of My Impulse to Bless and Liberate all-and-All.

However, My Conclusive Observation relative to all My Years of Divine Avataric Self-Submission is that My Blessing and Liberation of beings cannot be accomplished by Means of My Self-Submission.

Therefore, My Self-Submission need no longer be Done by Me.

Now, I Am Free of the Impulse to Submit Myself.

It was absolutely Necessary for Me to Make My Offering of Self-Submission.

It was absolutely Necessary that I Do <u>everything</u>, in order to See if My Blessing and Liberation of beings were possible by Means of My Self-Submission.

I have Demonstrated, with Absolute Conclusiveness, that Such is <u>not</u> possible.

Therefore, there is no purpose in any continuation of My Self-Submission.

Consequently, I am Standing Apart from the "world"— Living in Complete Freedom, in My Hermitage.

I do no institutional work of any kind.

I do no public work of any kind.

Fundamentally, I Live in the traditional manner, as Realizers (in all the time of the Ancient Walk-About Way) have lived in their hermitages.

I Am a Sapta Na Sannyasin, Utterly Free.

That Is It.

I Did My Submission-Work—and This Is How I now Am—<u>As</u> I <u>Am</u>.

I do not engage in any interactions with people on a social basis or an organizational basis.

I do not participate in mere ceremonialism.

I do not actively participate in any kind of "worldly" exchanges at any time with anyone.

I am simply present here, <u>As</u> I <u>Am</u>.

If people will devotionally respond to Me and relate to Me rightly, they can be invited to enter into My Divine Avataric Company for Blessing.

THE SELF-AUTHENTICATING TRUTH

Blessing Is simply My Nature, My State, My Intrinsic Condition of Self-Radiance.

Therefore, I do not have to engage in any kind of institutional ceremonialism in order to Bless.

If people will approach Me rightly, and searchlessly be in My Divine Avataric Company, they will, naturally, spontaneously, and inevitably, benefit from My Self-Radiant Company—because of the ego-transcending authenticity of their receptive devotional resort to Me.

The simple Sighting of Me is What is Effective in the case of all whose ego-transcending devotional recognition-response to Me is real and true.

It is up to those who are invited into My Company to be fully turned to Me, and to make use of the Blessed opportunity to be in My Divine Avataric Company.

My Instructions relative to all of this have been fully and plainly Given, and fully and plainly Written, by Me.

Therefore, My Divine Avataric Word must be studied, understood, and followed—without any intervening interpretation.

My Divine Avataric Self-Revelation Is Complete, Full, and Fully Stated.

I simply Live in My Hermitage—essentially solitary, not identified with the body or the mind, not egoically present here, but (rather) only egolessly, Transcendentally, and Spiritually Present.

My Standing Apart is Spiritually necessary and right— and It must be Done.

Therefore, It is now, and forever hereafter, Done by Me.

Now, and forever hereafter, I Stand Free Apart—and not in the middle—here.

The Way of Me

1.

My Avatarically Self-Revealed Divine Teaching-Word is <u>essentially</u> simple. I Say: Attend to <u>Me</u>—and (thus and thereby) understand and transcend your "self"-attending activity.

If any one will feel and examine his or her (psychophysical) state in any moment, whether under the worst or under the best or under the most ordinary of circumstances, he or she will surely discover that there is always a characteristic feeling of stress, or dis-ease, or a motivating sense of dilemma. Therefore, human life (characteristically felt as such stress, dis-ease, or dilemma) is also always characterized by struggle, or a generally uninspected (and never finally satisfied) search for release and fulfillment.

The usual life is always actively involved (whether consciously or unconsciously) in this motivated search and this native distress. Therefore, every such a one is involved in ego-based (or psycho-physically "self"-contracted) programs of seeking (via desire, in all kinds of relations and circumstances).

My Avatarically Self-Revealed Divine Teaching-Word Is a Direct Address to the distress and the search of each individual. I do not suggest a way (or a "method") by which to <u>seek</u>. Instead, I Call the individual to responsively and freely turn to Me, and, in that turning, to feel beyond the distress that would (otherwise) motivate the life of seeking itself.

Through the (necessarily, formal) practice of the only-by-Me Revealed and Given Way of Adidam (really and truly engaged as really ego-surrendering, and truly ego-forgetting, and directly ego-transcending heart-Communion with Me), and (in the constant context of that formal practice of devotionally Me-recognizing and devotionally to-Me-responding heart-Communion with Me) through real "consideration" of My Avatarically Given Divine Heart-Confessions, My Avatarically Given Divine Teaching-Arguments, My Avatarically Given Divine Image-Art, and the Recorded and Remembered Life-Stories of all My Avatarically Self-Manifested Divine Transcendental Spiritual Work (Whereby I have Reflected individuals to themselves, and Blessed them to Awaken)— individuals who truly devotionally recognize Me, and truly devotionally respond to Me, and (altogether) truly are devoted to Me can (by Means of My Avatarically Self-Transmitted Divine Transcendental Spiritual Grace) come to understand (and transcend) themselves, and (Ultimately) to Most Perfectly Realize Me (<u>As</u> Who and What they, and everyone, and everything, Really and Truly <u>Are</u>).

At first (in the Listening course of the only-by-Me Revealed and Given Way of Adidam), the individual becomes tacitly aware of his or her habits of seeking, desiring, doubting, believing, manipulating, betraying, and always returning to the same distress and want. In that tacit "self"-awareness, it is self-evident that all of that seeking is being motivated by a constant feeling of distress, which is the result of "self"-contraction in the face of all relations and conditions.

This discovery is most profound. It is as if a person in pain suddenly discovers that he or she is pinching his or her own flesh. (And this discovery produces immediate relief, as soon as the pinching ceases.) Therefore, as soon as an individual discovers that the painful search that occupies his or her life is being created by a fundamental feeling of distress, attention is free to examine that distress itself. And, when that distress is directly (and profoundly) examined, it is discovered that it is the result of a chronic (and "self"-induced) contraction of the body-mind, or, most simply, the habitual (and, ultimately, always voluntary and un-necessary) avoidance (or psycho-physically "self"-contracting refusal) of psycho-physical relationship and psycho-physical relatedness.

Every apparent individual, thing, circumstance, or condition arises, survives, changes, and disappears dependently (or always already related) within the cosmic universe (which is continuous, whole, and all-containing). By definition (and in fact), there is not (nor can there be) any separate, "self"-contained, independent, or "self"-sufficient conditional individual, thing, circumstance, or event. However, by reaction to all apparent vulnerability, and, otherwise, by forgetting (or by failing to notice or intuit) the Whole (and the Inherently Perfect, Which Inherently Transcends even the Whole), the tendency of every conditionally manifested individual is to contract into (presumed) separateness, or a "self"-defended and "self"-contracted emotional, mental, psychic, physical, and social state of isolation, presumed independence, and dramatized want. This tendency is chronic in every one, and it is generally not even inspected, nor is it (even if inspected) most fundamentally understood. Therefore, every one seeks. And all seeking is inevitably frustrated. The "self"-contracting habit (itself) is not (and cannot ever be) transcended in (or by means of) the search, because the search is itself the dramatization of the "self"-contracting habit itself.

I Call every one who turns to Me devotionally to tacitly feel and (thus and thereby) to thoroughly observe and (merely by always turning to Me) to transcend the habit of egoity. Any one who truly (and, necessarily, formally) Listens to My Avatarically Self-Revealed Divine Teaching-Word and, by the Means I have Given (and always Give), fully (and, necessarily, formally) embraces the devotional and (in due course) Transcendental Spiritual practice of heart-Communion with Me, and (in That Context) the tacit observation of the ego-"I", will surely (truly, and most profoundly) discover and transcend the "root" of seeking and suffering, which is the ego-"I" itself (or the psycho-physical "self"-contraction, which is the habit of "Narcissus", or the complex avoidance of relationship).

When this process (of devotionally turning to Me, and, thus and thereby, tacitly feeling beyond "self"-contraction) is truly and fully established and consistently enacted (relative, summarily, to every aspect of personal existence), a moment to moment event of spontaneous (and not strategic) release is enjoyed. And, when (in this Manner) the "self"-contraction-based life of seeking is tacitly relinquished, it becomes possible (in every moment of heart-Communion with Me) to engage the preliminary practice of "Reverse Enquiry", and (thus, by Means of the total practice of devotional turning to Me, right-life obedience to Me, and preliminary "Perfect Knowledge" of Me), to (more and more) enjoy a tacit sense of Inherent Freedom (and Fullness of Being). And any devotee of Mine who (necessarily, formally) practices the only-by-Me Revealed and Given Way of Adidam, and who has (through devotionally Me-recognizing and devotionally to-Me-responsive Listening to Me and, in due course, whole bodily Transcendental Spiritual Communion with Me) become fully responsible (and formally accountable) for this actively ego-transcending (or directly counter-egoic) feeling-capability, and who (thus and thereby) most fundamentally understands the "self"-contraction that is ego-"I", has Heard Me truly.

2.

During the Years of My Own Ordeal of Transcendental Spiritual Re-Awakening—or My total Ordeal of Establishing My Always Prior and Inherent Divine Self-Nature, Self-Condition, and Self-State of Transcendental Spiritual Awakening within the Context of My Divinely Avatarically-Born human Life-time—I spontaneously Developed the total process of the understanding (and the transcending) of the ego. All of My "Years of Testing-by-experience" eventually became a "Perfect Practice", and That "Perfect Practice" quickly brought My Ordeal of Re-Awakening to an end. Nevertheless, even all of My "Years of Testing-by-experience" were founded on the same basic Insight (or Heart-Awakening), and all those Years were punctuated by sudden Great Moments of Awakening and sudden Great Leaps of Understanding.

One such (and early) Incident of Heart-Awakening occurred quite gently (but most profoundly), in a moment in which I was mindlessly regarding My right hand, observing the (apparent and, suddenly, revealing) contrast between the natural (or open and functionally relational) attitude of the hand and the unnatural (or contracted and functionally dissociated) attitude of the clenched fist.

The natural sign of the human body is relatedness, not separateness and independence!

Therefore, when this sign convicted the heart, the subjective commitment to "self"-contraction was spontaneously released. In that moment, there was a quiet revolution in the body-mind. I "Knew" the "Always Already" State. And this began a period of Enquiry into the "self"-contraction (which appears, in action, as the avoidance of relationship). In due course, the Perfect (Tacit, Intrinsic, and Prior) Transcending of "self"-contraction became a constant "Perfect Practice" (of "Perfect Contemplation"), until, when the efforts and the effects of the avoidance of relationship (and every subjective

THE SELF-AUTHENTICATING TRUTH

trace of "self"-contraction) were Perfectly (or Priorly and Inherently) Transcended, there is the Tacit Certainty and Self-Illumined Awakeness of "I Am Conscious Light—I Am the One and the Only, the Real and Self-Existing and Self-Radiant, or 'Bright', Nature, Condition, and State of Transcendental, and Inherently Spiritual, Inherently egoless, and Self-Evidently Divine Being Itself".

My earliest and most basic Practice was an example of what is traditionally called "prapatti"—or simple, direct, non-technical, and unconditional surrender to Whatever Is Always Already The Case (without any believed concept of "What" That Is, or any previously acquired commitment to any specific means to be employed). It was not a practice informed by any conventional "religious" philosophy, or by any traditional Spiritual philosophy, or by any inherited "God"-concepts. (As a result of a profound intellectual and emotional crisis, I had despaired of all the "religious" and philosophical conventions that were proposed to Me in My Youth.) All that was possible for Me was the Real Practice of Divine Ignorance, or spontaneous (random, general, and unpredictable) Submission to the Un-"known" and Un-"knowable" (and, yet, Necessarily and Intrinsically Realizable) Nature, Condition, and State of Reality Itself—in and As Which the conditional "self" and the conditional "world" are arising in every moment.

I soon Enjoyed a profoundly essential Insight into the felt dilemma and the urge to seek that characterize the born (or conditional, and psycho-physical) "self". It became clear to Me that the feeling of dilemma and the urge to seek God, Happiness, Fulfillment, or Release via the acquisition of "experience", "knowledge", or any condition (or conditional "object") at all are not, in fact, the means for the Realization of Truth Itself. I Understood that the problem-feeling and the urge to seek are not a program for the actual discovery of Truth, but they are merely symptoms of a curious disease. I observed that these symptoms, which tend to characterize every moment of ordinary existence, are, in fact, the evidence of the very state that must be transcended if the Truth Itself is to be Realized. It was clear to Me that the feeling of dilemma and the seeking-urge are nothing more than a confession that God, or Truth, or Happiness is not presently "experienced" or "known". And this seemed remarkable to Me.

If God, or Truth, or Happiness is sought on the basis of a problem (or the feeling of dilemma), then God, or Truth, or Happiness is always projected into future time, and the Realization of God, or Truth, or Happiness is made conditional, or dependent upon psycho-physical events. This stood out to Me as nonsense, or as an absurd proposition.

My Own "Consideration" was this: God, or Truth, or Happiness must (Necessarily) Be Reality Itself, or That Which Is (Necessarily) Always Already The Case. Therefore, I observed that the felt dilemma and the urge to seek are simply the absurd confession that God, or Truth, or Happiness is absent now. And I observed further that the signs of dilemma and seeking are not a program for the actual future (or eventual, and future-time) Realization of God, or Truth, or Happiness, but they are merely a means for preventing actual Present (or Inherent, and present-time) Realization of God, or Truth, or Happiness. The feeling of dilemma and the urge to seek are actually the evidence of a disease, which is the conditional (or psycho-physical) "self" in its chronic contraction upon itself, and in its symptomatic non-Realization of Reality Itself (Which Is, Itself, God, or Truth, or Happiness).

Indeed, it became clear to Me that the "ego" (or the conventional "I") is not an "entity" (or an independent and static "thing of being"), but the "ego" (or the conventional "I") is the chronic and total psycho-physical activity of "self"-contraction, always associated with concrete results (in the psyche, mind, emotion, body, and their relations). And the "self"-contraction can always be tacitly observed (in any moment) in feeling (as fear, anxiety, stress, and all other kinds of reactive emotions and blocks in the flow of natural bodily energy in the Circle of the body-mind).

It became clear to Me that the "self"-contraction is the complex limit on natural bodily energy, and (in the case of the degrees and stages of Transcendental Spiritual Awakening) on the Divine Transcendental Spiritual Energy, in the Circle of the body-mind. Therefore, the "self"-contraction is (ultimately) a complex limit on the Inherent and Self-Existing Spiritual Radiance of Transcendental Divine Being, or the One and Indivisible and Intrinsically egoless Conscious Light That Is Reality Itself. And Perfect Freedom, or Inherent Happiness, or Inherently Most Perfect Real-God-Realization Is a matter of direct (or Inherent, or Most Prior) and Inherently Most Perfect (and Inherently Most Perfectly ego-Transcending) Self-Identification with the Self-Existing and Self-Radiant Nature, Condition, and State of Transcendental, Inherently Spiritual, Inherently egoless, and Self-Evidently Divine Being (or Self-Existing and Self-Radiant Conscious Light), Which Self-Identification is allowed only (in due course) by the real practice of always present-time (and, in due course, Most Perfect) transcending of the ego-act of "self"-contraction.

It became clear to Me that the "self"-contraction is unnecessary. The "self"-contraction is (without ultimate necessity, and, therefore, only apparently) being "added" to Existence Itself (in reaction to cosmic Nature, or to apparent conditional existence). The "self"-contraction (originally) coincides with and (effectively) perpetuates the apparition of cosmic Nature itself—and the presumption that Existence Itself is merely conditional (or merely apparent), and not founded on (and, altogether, dependent upon—and, Ultimately, characterized by) the Dimension of Non-conditionality (or of Non-conditional Existence). Therefore, the "self"-contraction is (originally—and, also, in effect, or conditionally) un-natural, because it superimposes on the Transcendental, and Inherently Spiritual, Divine Self (or Self-Existing and Self-Radiant Consciousness Itself) a false view of both cosmic Nature (or conditional reality) and the Divine Reality (or the Most Prior, and Entirely Non-conditional, and Intrinsically egoless Self-Nature, Self-Condition, Source-Condition, and Self-State That Is Reality Itself).

It became clear to Me that, when what is un-necessarily superimposed on Reality is released, What Stands (or Remains) As the Obvious Is (Necessarily, or Self-Evidently) Reality Itself, or the Real Condition Itself.

That is to say, Whatever Is Always Already The Case Authenticates Itself (Directly, Inherently, Obviously, and Perfectly).

Therefore, the transcending of egoity necessarily allows the Self-Revelation of the Transcendental, and Inherently Spiritual, Self-Nature, Self-Condition, Source-Condition, and Self-State As the Self-Authenticating (or Inherently and Obviously Real and True) and Most Prior (or Self-Evidently Divine) Reality and Truth!

This Heart-Awakened Insight was, in My Own Case, instantly Liberating! And, as such, It became the real practicing basis for the (at last, Most Perfect) Revelation (or Re-Realization) of My Own (Inherent, Self-Existing, Self-Radiant, Inherently egoless, and Self-Evidently Divine) Nature, Condition, and State—Which Is Reality, Truth, and Happiness!

The Insight Itself (or the Unique and Inherently Liberating Understanding Re-Awakened at the Heart) directly coincided (or arose simultaneously) with a Practice That was thereafter to be the most basic Characteristic of the Way of My Life (and Which was to Re-Awaken Full and Most Ultimate Realization). That Practice had two principal aspects. The first was profound Submission of attention and all the energies of the body-mind to observe, feel, and feel beyond the "self"-contraction. And the second, which coincided with the first and Ultimately Superseded it, was Direct Communion (and, Ultimately, Inherent Self-Identification) with the Prior Nature, Condition, and State That is Simply and Directly Obvious when the "self"-contraction is transcended (or no longer effective as a mechanism of dissociation from What <u>Is</u> Always Already <u>The</u> Case).

I observed that the sense (or feeling) of "absence", or the sense (or feeling) of the non-Presence of God, or the sense (or feeling) of separation from God, Truth, Happiness, or What cannot even be described, is not evidence of the real absence of God, Truth, Happiness, or the Indescribable, but it is clear evidence that the conditional "self" is contracting, or actively separating from What (Simply, Merely, or Really) <u>Is</u>.

I Named this disease (or the diseased "self") "Narcissus", because of the likeness between this "self"-program and the ancient myth of Narcissus. And I became attentive in every moment to this feeling of absence, of separateness, of dilemma, and the urge to seek.

Remarkably, in every moment of such observation, I felt the non-necessity (as well as the deluding, or binding, effect) of the "self"-contraction—such that a spontaneous release occurred in every such moment. That is to say, I observed that it was un-necessary to presume or suffer or be motivated by the "self"-contraction in any moment of My direct observation of it. And, in that observation, a deep spontaneous response of "self"-release was Awakened. And, whenever that release of "self"-contraction occurred, That Which Is Always Already The Case (Previous, and Most Prior, to "self"-contraction) Stood Out As the Obvious.

In due course, What <u>Is</u> (Previous, and Most Prior, to "self"-contraction) was Revealed most profoundly. And, in the course of That Revelation, there was also the spontaneous manifesting of the many extraordinary phenomena that are characteristic of each of the seven stages of life.

The Process of That Revelation by stages was not founded <u>only</u> on the basis of Insight (or "self"-Understanding) and the spontaneous transcending of egoity, or what I Call the "'conscious process'", but It was <u>equally</u> (or always coincidently) associated with a Response to What was being Revealed. Thus, It also involved what I Call "Seeing"—or fullest (and Transcendentally Spiritually Activated, and, Transcendentally Spiritually, fully technically responsible) emotional (and total psycho-physical) conversion to true (and truly responsible) "conductivity" (and spontaneous, and total psycho-physical, Self-Identification with the Inherent Love-Bliss-Condition) of the Transcendental Spirit-Power (and Inherently egoless Transcendental Spiritual Nature, Condition, and State) of the Divine Acausal Self-"Brightness".

What <u>Is</u> (Always and Already) is Revealed <u>only</u> when the "self"-contraction is not effective. What <u>Is</u> (Always and Already) is Revealed to Be Self-Radiant (or Inherently Spiritual), and Self-Existing (or Transcendental), and Inherently egoless, and Self-Evidently Divine Being, or Conscious Light—Which <u>Is</u> Reality Itself, Truth Itself, and Happiness Itself. Any and every conditionally manifested "I" Always Already Inheres in That Self-Evidently Divine Self-Nature, Self-Condition, and Self-State, both at the Level of Self-Existing Being (or Consciousness Itself) and at the level of every apparent (or conditionally manifested) psycho-physical function, process, or state. Even the body-mind is only an apparent modification of That Self-Existing "Bright" Divine Self-Radiance in Which every "I" is arising.

When This Realization was Most Perfectly Re-Awakened in My Own Case—all beings, this "world", and all the kinds of other "worlds" were Revealed in <u>Me</u>, Inhering in <u>Me</u>, and appearing as (apparent) modifications of <u>Me</u>! And it became Self-Evidently Clear that, by virtue of My Own Inherently Most Perfect Divine Self-Realization of My Own Divine Self-Nature, Self-Condition, and Self-State, <u>all</u> (apparently "other") conditionally manifested beings (now, and forever hereafter) can—by Means of their devotionally Me-recognizing and devotionally to-Me-responding heart-devotion to Me—Realize What (and Who) Is Reality, Truth, and Happiness!

Suddenly and Spontaneously, What I had forgotten by progressive life-Submission after Birth was, by Me, Remembered in the midst of life itself—and the Avataric Significance and Divine Purpose of My Own Birth became Clear, again, to Me: I Am the One Who Is Always Already The Case, and even all beings Are in Me (Ultimately, Beyond all "difference")!

When This Truth (and Condition) became (to Me) Obvious (As Truth, and As My Condition), the Avatarically Self-Transmitting Powers of My Transcendental, Inherently Spiritual, Inherently egoless, and Self-Evidently Divine Person Spontaneously became Active in and As My Divinely Self-Manifested (and Avatarically-Born—or, Avatarically, conditionally Shown) bodily (human) Divine Form, and My Avatarically Self-Transmitted Transcendental Spiritual (and Always all-and-All-Blessing) Divine Presence, and My Perfectly Subjective (and Very, and Inherently egoless, and Inherently Perfect, and Self-Evidently Divine, and Avatarically Self-Revealed) State! And I became Heart-Moved to forever Avatarically Serve the Most Perfect Divine Awakening of the total Cosmic Mandala of conditionally manifested beings!

In the course of My Own Ordeal of Spiritual, Transcendental, and Divine Self-Realization (or Re-Awakening, in the Context of My Divinely Avatarically-Born human Lifetime), the Great (ego-Transcending) Capability That always Informed My Practice was a constant Divine Avataric Demonstration of the great (and most fundamental) capability that must awaken to characterize the practice of anyone who (by heart, and in the Way of Adidam) will Realize the Living (or Inherently Spiritual) and Transcendental Divine Truth of Reality Itself. That great and most fundamental capability, which is (at last) Perfected in Most Perfect Divine Self-Realization, matures from (or on the basis of) the original and spontaneous urge to observe and transcend the "self"-contraction. And that great and most fundamental capability (awakened on the basis of thorough "self"-observation) expresses the clear (and most fundamental) understanding that the "self"-contraction (and not the real absence of Real Acausal God, or Reality, or Truth, or Happiness) is the only reason why Real-God-Communion (or Ecstatic, Tacit, and Direct Realization of Real Acausal God, or Reality, or Truth, or Happiness Itself, or the Real Condition That Is Always Already The Case) is not enjoyed in the present. This Heart-Awakened Insight, and the Great Capability for spontaneous release that extends from It, were the ground of My (at last) Free Surrender—and That Surrender was not encumbered or retarded by dilemma, nor was That Surrender made fruitful by the search toward any goal.

I was not born to be projected toward the future. I was Avatarically Born—to Self-Reveal My Own Inherently ego-less and Self-Evidently Divine Self-Nature, Self-Condition, and Self-State, As That Which Is Always Already The Case in every moment. Therefore, even in My Own Case, the process—of ecstatic (or ego-transcending) Communion (and, at last, Inherent Self-Identification) with That Which is (in every moment of the transcending of egoity) Divinely Self-Revealed (Self-Evidently, As That Which Is Always Already The Case)—manifested, spontaneously and inevitably, as a transcending of the characteristic signs of each of the first six stages of life, and (Ultimately) the unfolding of the characteristic signs of the only-by-Me Revealed and Given seventh stage of life.

Such Is the Nature of the Process in My Own (Avatarically-Born) Case.

Such Is the Nature of the Process of ego-transcending and Me-Realizing devotion to Me.

Such Is the Nature and the Process of the Way That Only I Reveal and Give.

The Unique and Priorly egoless Reality-Way of Sighting Me and Listening To Me

1.

The only-by-Me Revealed and Given Reality-Way of Adidam is the Way of Sighting Me and Listening to Me.

The only-by-Me Revealed and Given Reality-Way of Adidam does not proceed by the traditional conventional means of "problem" (or of "question") and of seeking-"method".

The only-by-Me Revealed and Given Reality-Way of Adidam is not initiated by an address (or an "answer") to the mind—nor does the practice develop by means of bodily, emotional, mental, or otherwise psycho-physically exercised means (or seeking-"methods") that are strategically intended to solve any "problem" or to imitate or animate any ideal.

2.

The Way of Sighting Me and Listening to Me is a "radical" (or always "at-the-root") practice.

The Way of Sighting Me and Listening to Me is an intrinsically ego-transcending practice.

The Way of Sighting Me is the devotional practice of whole bodily (or total psycho-physical) recognition-response to the Intrinsically and Perfectly Me-Revealing Sight (and the

Transcendental Spiritual Self-Radiance-Transmission) of My Avatarically-Born bodily (human) Divine Form—such that, by That recognition-responsive Me-Sighting alone, whole bodily turning and surrendering to My Divinely Avatarically (and Transcendentally Spiritually) Self-Revealed egoless Self-Nature, Self-Condition, and Self-State is spontaneously, inevitably, and constantly (moment to moment) demonstrated.

Right and true (and truly ego-forgetting, ego-surrendering, and ego-transcending) devotional Sighting of Me is the Divinely Avatarically-Given Way of tacit participatory Self-Apprehension (or Self-Apperception) of the egoless Transcendental Spiritual and Self-Evidently Divine Self-Nature, Self-Condition, and Self-State of Reality Itself.

The Way of Listening to Me follows upon and entirely develops from the right and true devotional practice of Sighting Me.

The Way of Listening to Me is the already and constantly (moment to moment) Me-Sighting, Me-recognizing, and whole bodily to-Me-responsive devotional practice of ego-forgetting, ego-surrendering, and ego-transcending "root"-receptivity to the vocalized and audible (or, otherwise, for the sake of the deaf, visually signed, or even, for the deaf-and-blind, touch-signed) Recitation of My Divinely Avatarically Self-Revealing Reality-Word—and, entirely and only by that whole bodily ego-forgetting, ego-surrendering, and ego-transcending Me-receptive sensory-based Listening to My Divinely Avatarically Self-Revealing Reality-Word, tacitly Self-"Locating" the egoless and Self-Evidently Divine Self-Nature, Self-Condition, and Self-State That Is Reality Itself.

In due course, the Way of Sighting Me and Listening to Me becomes moment to moment ego-forgetting, ego-surrendering, ego-transcending, and truly searchless Me-Beholding—and, Thus and Thereby, the only-by-Me Revealed and Given (and always Me-Sighting and to-Me-Listening) Reality-Way of Adidam matures into a Transcendental Spiritual and (in due course) Perfectly Reality-Realizing Way of devotional Communion with Me.

3.

The Way of Sighting Me and Listening to Me is not a seeking-"method" for "causing" the transformation, the fulfillment, or even the transcending of the psycho-physical ego-"I".

The Way of Sighting Me is simply That—to Sight (and, as even the blind may do, to whole-bodily-feel the Transcendental Spiritual Presence Self-Radiated by and <u>As</u>) My Tacitly and Acausally Reality-Revealing bodily (human) Divinely Avataric Form—such that the total psycho-physical reaction-activity of "self"-contraction (or the reactive assertion of egoic separateness and separativeness) is not enacted, but is (rather) Priorly relinquished, vanished, and effectively renounced, in the whole-bodily-heart-intelligent devotional event of ego-forgetting, ego-surrendering, and ego-transcending Me-Sighting.

The Way of Listening to Me is simply That—to Listen to My Divinely Avatarically Self-Revealing Reality-Word, Spoken Aloud (or, by one or another sensory means, Recited or otherwise Communicated) to the "ear" of heart—in such a manner that the heart-intelligent total body is openly and freely receptive to My Word at the "root"-depth, Prior to the egoic "self"-contraction of the psycho-physical faculties.

4.

Right and true Sighting of Me and Listening to Me is a searchless and constant (moment to moment) devotional orientation of the heart-intelligent total body, and not merely an exercise of the body-mind on the basis of the already "self"-contracted orientation of ego-"I", its "problems", or its will to seeking.

Right and true Sighting of Me is a searchless and constant (moment to moment) devotional process of heart-intelligent whole bodily recognition-response to My Divinely Avatarically Self-Revealed whole-bodily-egoless and Transcendentally Spiritually Self-Radiant Self-Nature, Self-Condition, and Self-State—and (Thus and Thereby) tacitly (prior to verbal thinking) and whole-bodily-responsively Communing with and (as a heart-intelligent bodily totality) participating in My Divinely Avatarically Self-Revealed whole-bodily-egoless and Transcendentally Spiritually Self-Radiant Self-Nature, Self-Condition, and Self-State.

Right and true Listening to Me is not the search to mentally (or verbally) understand (or, altogether, to merely conditionally and egoically "know") Me by reading, and thinking about, and talking about, and, altogether (by egoic and conditionally-projected means), "objectifying" My Divinely Avatarically Self-Revealing Reality-Word—but, rather, right and true Listening to Me is the intrinsically ego-forgetting, ego-surrendering, and ego-transcending devotional practice and process of silent (and prior to verbal thinking) heart-Listening (or heart-intelligent whole bodily receptivity) to My Divinely Avatarically Self-Revealing Reality-Word by Means of Its Recitation.

Right and true Listening to Me is tacit (silent and pre-verbal) heart-attentiveness to the Intrinsic and Non-"Objective" Silence of My Divinely Avatarically Reality-Revealing Self-Nature, Self-Condition, and Self-State—As I Am (Thus, and <u>As</u> Such) Self-Communicated and Self-Revealed by the Acausal Self-Transmission of My egolessly Self-Revealing Divine Avataric Reality-Word.

Therefore, the devotional practice of right and true Listening to the Recitation of My Divinely Avatarically Self-Revealing Reality-Word is the tacit (silent and pre-verbal), whole bodily heart-attentive, and Intrinsically ego-transcending Reality-practice of Listening to My Own Silence—Which <u>Is</u> the Transcendental Spiritual Essence of <u>all</u> heard speech.

Thus, even though the practice of reading, systematically studying, thinking about, and talking about My Divinely Avatarically Self-Revealing Word has its necessary use as a basic practical support for right and true practice of the Way of Sighting Me and Listening to Me, the fundamental right and true practice of Listening to Me is engaged as a tacitly (silently and non-verbally, and even pre-verbally) heart-intelligent whole bodily devotional receptivity-practice, wherein My Divinely Avatarically Self-Revealed (and Intrinsically Reality-Revealing) Word is neither addressed to nor received by nor mediated by the mind (or even by the total psycho-physical ego-"I", or "self"-contraction altogether), but is, rather, tacitly received At, and In, and By the "Root"-and-Prior Depth—or tacitly and directly, by the inherently thought-free nervous system and brain as a whole, and, Prior to all thought or bodily action, At, and In, and By the egoless Transcendental, Spiritual, and Self-Evidently Divine Self-Nature, Self-Condition, and Self-State That Always Already Is, Prior to egoic "self"-identification with the body-mind.

Therefore, the constantly-Sighting-Me-and-Listening-to-Me culture of the only-by-Me Revealed and Given Reality-Way of Adidam is an intensively ego-forgetting, ego-surrendering, and ego-transcending culture of tacit, heart-intelligent, whole bodily devotional attendance to Me and receptivity to Me—wherein the fundamental practices are those of the devotional formal Sighting of My Avatarically-Born bodily (human) Divine Form and the devotional Listening to the formal Recitation of My Divinely Avatarically Self-Revealing and Reality-Revealing Word.

The Essentials of Reality-Practice
In The Way of Adidam

1.

Until The "Perfect Practice"

More and more Perfectly Self-Abide <u>As</u> That Which is not an "object" (and, therefore, not the body-mind), by devotionally surrendering the total body-mind to My Divinely Avatarically-Born bodily (human) Form, My Always-Blessing Transcendental Spiritual Presence, and My Very and Inherently egoless State.

Do This until Perfect and Non-conditional and Steady Transcendental Spiritual Awakening to The Witness-State, Prior to all "objects" and all egoic "self"-identification with the body-mind.

2.

In The "Perfect Practice"

The "Perfect Practice" is egoless Transcendental Spiritual Self-Abiding <u>As</u> That Which <u>Is</u> egolessly Prior to body, mind, and all "objects".

The "Perfect Practice" <u>Is</u> The egoless Perfect Disposition Itself.

The egoless Perfect Disposition is not, Itself, characterized by either "yes" or "no" relative to body, mind, or any "object" or state of body and/or mind.

The egoless Perfect Disposition, Itself, simply has no association with, no reaction to, and no "issues" about body, mind, or any "object" or state of body and/or mind.

The egoless Perfect Disposition Merely Stands Free—Prior to all egoic "self"-identification with body, mind, and any "object" or state of body and/or mind.

In due course, The "Perfect Practice" becomes seventh stage egoless Transcendental Spiritual Self-Abiding, Divinely Self-Recognizing all apparent "objects" (and the total body-mind) As egoless Self-Conscious Transcendental Spiritual Love-Bliss—and, thus, as merely apparent modifications of The Prior Indivisible egoless Conscious Light That Is Reality itself.

On That egoless Perfect Basis, Merely Self-Abide, Divinely Self-Recognizing (and, Thus, Priorly and Perfectly Self-Transcending) all-and-All that apparently arises—Until The Prior Indivisible egoless Conscious Light That Is Reality Itself Perfectly Outshines all-and-All.

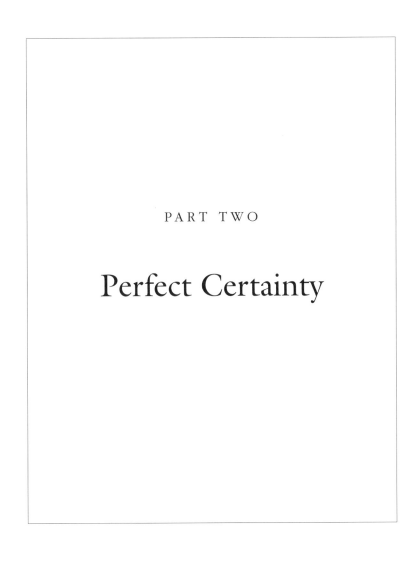

PART TWO

Perfect Certainty

The Perfectly Non-Objective
Way of Adidam

1.

Reality Itself is not an "object".
Reality Itself <u>Is</u> Not-an-"object".

2.

In and <u>As</u> Reality Itself:
  There is no "objective" or separate "universe".
  There is no "objective" or separate "self".
  There <u>Is</u> No-separateness.
  There is no "objective" or separate "other".
  There <u>Is</u> No-otherness.
  There are no "objective" or separate "relations".
  There <u>Is</u> No-relatedness.
  There are no "objective" or separate "differences".
  There <u>Is</u> No-"difference".

3.

Any and every presumption of separateness, relatedness, otherness, or "difference" is an extension or a reflection of a dissociative state of non-coincidence with Reality Itself.

Any and every "experience" of separateness, relatedness, otherness, or "difference" is a psycho-physical illusion, generated by a reflexive contraction-reaction of body and/or mind.

4.

The only-by-Me Revealed and Given Reality-Way of Adidam is a process of Non-"objective" understanding.

The only-by-Me Revealed and Given Reality-Way of Adidam Is the Intrinsically and Always Priorly ego-transcending practice of Not-an-"object".

In the only-by-Me Revealed and Given seventh stage of life in The Reality-Way of Adidam, any and every instance of the arising of apparent or otherwise conventionally presumed separateness, relatedness, otherness, or "difference" is Priorly and Perfectly Self-Recognized In and As The egoless and Non-"objective" Self-Nature, Self-Condition, and Self-State of Reality Itself.

The only-by-Me Revealed and Given seventh stage of life in The Reality-Way of Adidam Is The egoless Transcendental Spiritual and Self-Evidently Divine Self-Awakening of The egoless, Indivisible, Acausal, and Perfectly Non-"objective" Self-Nature, Self-Condition, and Self-State of Reality Itself— Always Already Perfectly Prior to separateness, relatedness, otherness, and "difference".

Reality Itself Is <u>Not</u> In The Middle

1.

The scientific description of light as an appearance characterized by both "particles" and "waves" is further explained (and unified) if light is understood (and observed) to be always in a spiral (or helix) form—like the material form of DNA (which is, itself, a direct materialization of the structure of light).

If a spiral-form is seen at its point of rotation (or its crossover joint), it is observable as a "particle"—and if the same spiral-form is seen with reference to its limbs of rotation (before or after its point of rotation, or its crossover joint), it is observable as a "wave".

So, also, light is observable as both "particle" and "wave"—depending on which phase of its process is observed by attention (or "point of view", or ego-"I") in time and space.

A vibrating string can be seen to demonstrate the same spiraliform gait as any mode of observable light—and, so, as a kind of poetic inspiration, modern scientists have proposed numerous "string theories", in their search for the "knowledge" that will "explain everything".

Nevertheless, whether light is observed (and, thus, understood) as a "particle" or as a "wave" or as a "string", that observation (or understanding) is, itself, an act of <u>perspectival</u> "<u>objectification</u>", wherein and whereby Reality Itself is reduced—by the very act of observation, or understanding, or mental fabrication—to a <u>relation</u> (and, thus, a subordinate) of attention, or "point of view", or ego-"I".

The ancient and modern perspectival "objectification" of Reality Itself as either "Deity", or "self", or "world" has historically extended the naive illusion (or naive "realism", or ego-based illusionism) of separateness, relatedness, otherness, and "difference" that is inherent to the space-time "self"-locatedness of attention, or "point of view", or ego-"I".

2.

An "object" is (or appears as) an "object" only because it is being perceived or conceived from a "point of view" in space and time.

Therefore, What Is the Nature, Condition, or State of an "object" when "it" is not being viewed from any "point of view" in space and time?

Apart from "point of view", are there any "objects" (as such)—or any "differences" at all?

Or, rather, if all possible "objects" (or "differences") are simultaneously existing—as they must be, unless and until "point of view" differentiates and particularizes them—then What Is the Nature, Condition, or State of that simultaneous totality?

The "world" of memory and perception and all of thinking is a "point-of-view"-fabrication.

The "experientially" (and, thus, conditionally) "known world" is brain's illusion of "out there", devised by attention's perspective and made important by the persistence of ego-"I" (or the presumption of separate "self").

Apart from the defining and categorizing done by ego-"I", What Is That Totality Beyond perspective, and thought, and every now of time, and every place of space-"locatedness"?

That "What" Is The Only "Universe" That Really Is.

And no brain-made mind or body-"self" can say That "Universe" is seen by any ego-"I" at any time or place.

3.

The search for "knowledge" is hunter-gatherer behavior, based on the ancient pre-"civilized" brain.

The search for "knowledge" leads to "Scapegoat" (or "object-in-the-middle") rituals, in which power is <u>always</u> exercised over the "middle" (even to the degree of destroying it).

Reality Itself is <u>not</u> in the "middle".

Reality Itself <u>Is</u> Inherently and Perfectly Prior to all-and-All.

Ancient "religious" humankind thought and actively believed that the Sun revolves around the Earth.

Reality Itself does <u>not</u> surround or "revolve around" attention, or "point of view", or ego-"I".

Modern "scientific" humankind thinks and actively believes that the Earth revolves around the Sun.

Attention, or "point of view", or ego-"I", does <u>not</u> surround or "revolve around" Reality Itself.

Reality Itself egolessly, Indivisibly, and Divinely <u>Is</u> <u>As</u> <u>Is</u>—always already Prior to attention, "point of view", and ego-"I".

Reality Itself <u>Is</u> Self-Evidently Divine.

Reality Itself <u>Is</u> The Only Divine.

Reality Itself is <u>not</u> a Deity.

Reality Itself is <u>not</u> a <u>relation</u> of attention, "point of view", or ego-"I".

Reality Itself—or The Divine Itself—<u>Is</u> The egoless and relationless Context of all-and-All.

The ancients thought What <u>Is</u> Divine to be a Deity—or <u>The</u> Great Relation of attention, "point of view", and ego-"I".

Over time, humankind subordinated "The Deity"—or "The Great Relation"—to attention, "point of view", and ego-"I".

Eventually, "The Deity"—or "The Great Relation"—was reduced to "Scapegoat" status, as a mere "object" of exploitation by attention, "point of view", and ego-"I".

At last, "The Deity"—or "The Great Relation"—was "scientifically" (and, thus and thereby, "officially") discarded, or relegated to the status of a non-thought, or a non-idea, or a mere illusion (not to be thought again).

In the course of the cultural, social, and political history of "The Deity"—or "The Great Relation" anciently invented by human thought—attention itself, or "point of view" itself, or the ego-"I" itself has, reductively and progressively (and, now, finally), become the Reality-Facsimile, and the Great Subject, and the Principal Occupation of humankind.

4.

It is—now and urgently—time for a new understanding of Reality Itself to emerge.

The old cultures of ego-based fabrications of Reality Itself and the reductionism of "point of view" have been disproved by the persistence of Reality Itself—Which refuses all human efforts to subordinate "It" to attention, "point of view", or ego-"I".

Neither attention itself, nor "point of view" itself, nor ego-"I" itself <u>Is</u> (in and of and as itself) Reality Itself.

Reality Itself <u>Is</u> That Which Inherently and Self-Evidently Transcends attention, "point of view", and ego-"I".

Reality Itself <u>Is</u> That Which Is Realizable only if and as attention, or "point of view", or ego-"I" is transcended in Reality Itself.

The Way of Realizing Reality Itself is <u>not</u> "religious"—or a path of seeking toward union (or re-unification) with Reality Itself conceived as a Deity.

The Way of Realizing Reality Itself is <u>not</u> "scientific"—or a path of seeking to "know" (and, thus and thereby, to control) Reality Itself conceived as a relation (and, as such, a subordinate) of attention, or of "point of view", or of ego-"I".

Reality Itself is <u>not</u> an "Object" or a "Goal" of attention, "point of view", or ego-"I".

Reality Itself is <u>not</u> "outside" attention, "point of view", or ego-"I".

Reality Itself is <u>not</u> "inside" attention, "point of view", or ego-"I".

Reality Itself <u>Is</u> The egoless Non-relation—or The Perfectly Prior, Acausal, and Indivisible Context—of all-and-All.

Reality Itself <u>Is</u> The Intrinsically Self-Evident and Self-Evidently Divine Self-Nature, Self-Condition, and Self-State of all apparent modes of "subject" (or of conditionally apparent consciousness) and all apparent modes of "object" (or of conditionally apparent light, or energy, or space, or time).

Reality Itself <u>Is</u> Indivisible Conscious Light Itself.

Reality Itself <u>Is</u> The Non-"Objective" and Non-"Iconic" Real God of all-and-All.

Reality Itself <u>Is</u> The Non-"Objective" and Indivisible Spiral and Sphere of egoless Conscious Light.

Reality Itself <u>Is</u> The Only Cure for the perennial epidemic of human "religious" and anti-"religious" psychoses.

All of the perennial human "religious" and anti-"religious" psychoses—whether personal, or social, or cultural, or political—are merely symptoms of egoity (or of the faults of attention, or "point of view"), which "cause" and, altogether, indicate the egoically reactive human refusal of The Intrinsic and Essential Self-Nature, Self-Condition, and Self-State of egoless and Non-"different" Inherence In and <u>As</u> Reality Itself.

Reality Itself is <u>not</u> in the "middle"—but Reality Itself <u>Is</u> That Acausal Omni-Presence In and <u>As</u> Which all-and-All arises as a merely apparent modification of <u>Itself</u>.

The Certainty Principle

The "uncertainty principle", upon which much of modern scientific theorizing depends, is proposed* on the basis of the circumspect observation that it is not possible to simultaneously observe (and, thus, to "know") both the speed and the location of a "particle" of light (or energy).

On the basis of this observation relative to the intrinsic limitations of any observing "point of view", modern scientific theorizing has developed complex analytical and mathematical tools of measurement (especially in the subatomic and quantum domain) that presume that light (or energy)—and, thus, the "universe itself"—is, itself, a paradoxical domain (or even a domain of multiple and parallel universes). As a consequence of such theorizing relative to the process of measurement, probability and possibility (rather than certainty) has become the context of both theory and measurement in the field of subatomic and quantum physics.

Whatever the conventional merits of such science may be, it must be understood that to "know" the speed and location of a "particle" (or anything else) is relevant only to "point of view" (or the would-be "knower" that is attention itself, "self"-located in time and space as a psycho-physically-defined ego-"I").

That is to say, the "uncertainty principle" applies to "point of view" (or any space-time-located observer)—but that does not indicate that Reality Itself can rightly be characterized by either the limitations or the presumed "knowledge" of "point of view" (or of the space-time-located observer) itself.

*The "uncertainty principle" mentioned here was formally proposed by German physicist Werner Heisenberg in 1927.

To "know" the spatial location of a "particle", the observing "point of view" must disregard its own process (of motion and change) in time—and, thus, in that instant, it cannot observe (because it does not assume either the position or the disposition to observe) the speed (or the time-process) of the any "particle". That is to say, only a "point of view" that is presumed to be located in and as a definite and specific (or fixed and unchanging) spatial "place" can, with certainty, predict or "know" the definite and specific location of a thereby observed "particle" (or anything else). Indeed, it may rightly be said that the presumed spatial locatedness of the "point of view" (or the observer) determines (or, by and with reference to itself, "causes") the definite and specific location of the "particle" (or the whatever)—which is even to say that spatial "location" is, itself, a physical (or body-"self") illusion (or, at best, a merely perspectival artifice, with reference to the always temporary and reductive, and, thus, illusory, presumption of a spatially fixed "point of view").

To "know" the speed (or motion, or change, in time) of a "particle", the observing "point of view" must disregard its own location in space—and, thus, in that instant, it cannot observe (because it does not assume either the position or the disposition to observe) the spatial location of the "particle". That is to say, only a "point of view" that is presumed to be located (and moving and changing) in time (and not merely fixed in a definite and specific spatial location) can, with certainty, measure or "know" the speed of motion and change of a thereby observed "particle" (or anything else). Indeed, it may rightly be said that "self"-identification with the time-based characteristic (of motion and change) by the observing "point of view" (and its consequent "self"-forgetting relative to the noticing of its own presumption of fixed spatial locatedness) determines (or, by and with reference to itself, "causes") the apparent speed of the motion and change (or even the fact of the motion and change) of the "particle" (or the whatever)—which is even to say that the speed, the motion itself, and the appearance of change observed in any instance is, itself, a <u>mental</u> (<u>or</u> <u>mind-"self"</u>) <u>illusion</u> (or, at best, a merely historical, or time-based, artifice, with reference to the always temporary and reductive, and, thus, illusory, presumption of a time-defined, and, thus, <u>time-bound</u>, "point of view").

In other words, the observability (or "knowability") of factors of either space or time depends on the orientation (or "self"-presumed "self"-characteristic) of the observing "point of view"—which cannot be both a space-oriented space-identity and a time-oriented temporal identity (or both a thoroughly physical "self" and a thoroughly mental "self") in the same instant.

However, this intrinsic limitation of the "knower" (or the alternately space-bound and time-bound, or alternately physically-bound and mind-bound, "point of view") is not an intrinsic limitation of Reality Itself—Which, Intrinsically, Is Always Already Perfectly and Simultaneously Coincident with (and Perfectly and Transcendentally, or limitlessly and egolessly, Identical to) <u>all</u> of space and <u>all</u> of time.

The implications of this understanding are that the "uncertainty principle" is based on a correct observation of (alternately) spatially and temporally limited "point of view" and of (alternately) spatially and temporally limited "point-of-view"-based "knowledge"—but it is not a correct basis for understanding Reality Itself (Which Is Intrinsically Free of "point of view", or "knowledge"-limitation, or separate "self"-identity and perspectival illusion with reference to Itself).

Reality Itself Intrinsically, Always Priorly, Necessarily, and Perfectly Transcends any and every space-time-located (and, thus, space-time-bound) "point of view" and all space-time-limited "point-of-view"-based "knowledge".

There are, intrinsically, an infinite number of possible locations for "point of view" in space or time. Each and every "point of view" is an alternative possibility of factual measure. Each and every "point of view" is irreducibly "self"-identical, and non-identical to any other "point of view". Each and every "point of view" is a limitation—intrinsically incapable of "knowing" the totality of universe. Therefore, each and every "point of view" suffers from intrinsic uncertainty relative to the exact and comprehensive and instant measuring of its context of space and time. Indeed, each and every "point of view" is, itself, a discrete and unique force and possibility of measurement—and, thus, each and every "point of view" conditions, limits, and (by and with reference to itself) "causes" the spatial and temporal characteristics of every "particle"-event (or space-time-event) it happens to observe.

The probability/possibility paradoxes of space-time measurement and the analytically invented presumptions about multiple and parallel (and intrinsically non-observable) universes that characterize modern scientific theorizing all arise on the basis (and as a consequence) of "point of view"—alternately "self"-located in either space or time, and intrinsically incapable of simultaneously measuring both the spatial and the temporal characteristics of any "particle"-event, and intrinsically incapable of measuring the simultaneous totality of the event of universe, and intrinsically incapable of measuring (or, by any conditional means, "knowing") The Self-Nature, The Self-Condition, and The Self-State of Reality Itself.

The probability/possibility paradoxes of space-time measurement and the analytically invented presumptions about multiple and parallel (and intrinsically non-observable) universes that characterize modern scientific theorizing pertain to the intrinsically limited (and ego-bound) domain of very human "knowledge"—but The Domain of Reality Itself Exceeds all such understandings.

Indeed, Reality Itself Is Beyond and Prior to all measuring by "point of view" in space and time—and, therefore, the scientific "knowledge" of the "known" universe (or universes) of psycho-physical attention is not a Reality-Picture of Reality Itself.

Reality Itself must be understood to Be (Itself) not based upon the "uncertainty principle" (and, thus, "knowable" only in terms of paradoxical measurements)—but Reality Itself must be understood to Be (Itself) The Principle of Absolute Non-"knowability" (or of Only Intrinsic Self-Apprehension, or "Perfect Knowledge", Always Already Prior to "point of view", or space-time-located attention, or the psycho-physically-based and only conventionally "knowing" ego-"I").

Reality Itself Is Certainly Not "knowable".

Conventional (or "point-of-view"-based) "knowledge" (or all "knowledge" presumed or attained on the basis of space-time-located "point of view" and its naive realism relative to what is perceived and/or thought) is, certainly, always and inherently based on fundamental uncertainty—or paradox-only.

The inference of multiple and parallel universes (as, for example, in the vast proposals of so-called "string theories") is, rather, a mere idea, or a paradoxical and abstract "picture" in the mind (and, indeed, a "picture" of what is otherwise both invisible and unobservable). The inference of multiple and parallel universes suggests there is a single, separate, and unique universe for each and every "particle"-event (or each and every possibility at all, or each and every variant of measurement of space or time, or each and every variant of "sames"). The experiential fact is not multiple (and alternative) universes, but the evident variable of "point of view"—which is not merely potentially multiple, but, rather, an infinite variable. Within the apparently observable universe of space and time, there are an infinite number of possible "points" from which the "view" may be taken. Therefore, every "particle" within the total universe is, potentially, "viewable" from an infinite number of either spatial or temporal "positions"—and each such "position" will "self"-create its own measurement relative to any "particle" it "views". The fact of inherently infinite possible variations on the measurements of speed and location relative to any "particle" is the fundamental basis for all uncertainty and all probability/possibility paradoxes. Relatively speaking, every "point of view" is the root-"cause" and center of a unique and independent universe of probability/possibility and uncertainty. That is to say, the root of all paradoxes of space-time measurement is not multiple actual universes but the actuality of an infinite number of possible "points of view".

It is not possible to "picture" (or otherwise exactly and comprehensively conceive in mind) The Infinite and Indivisible Self-Nature, Self-Condition, and Self-State of Reality Itself. Therefore, there cannot be a true "theory of everything".

Reality Itself is not multiplied (or ever stood parallel to Itself)—but "It" Is One and Indivisible.

Reality Itself is neither certain nor uncertain relative to conventional "knowledge"—but, rather, Reality Itself has nothing to do with conventional "knowledge" (or "point of view", or attention, or ego-"I", or space-time-locatedness of any kind).

Reality Itself Is The Simultaneous and Indivisible Totality of Everything-all-at-once—Which Is Perfectly and Always Already Prior to "point of view" (and space-time itself), and Which Is Non-separate and Non-conditional Conscious Light, Perfectly and Always Already Prior to all apparent and otherwise possible "differences".

Reality Itself Is The Intrinsically Certain Identity-Principle of Self-Existence—or of The Intrinsic Self-Apprehension of Self-Existence and Self-Radiance As Reality Itself and As One and Indivisible Conscious Light Itself.

Reality Itself Is Only Perfect Certainty—or The Intrinsic and Self-Evident Self-Certainty (or egoless Self-Apprehension) That Is "Perfect Knowledge" Only.

Reality Itself <u>Is</u> Real God

1.

A ll change is process.
All process is measured by "difference", observed in the context (or mental language) of time.

All change, or process, or "difference", or time is a measure relative to "point of view".

Unless a "point of view" is assumed, no change, or process, or "difference", or time is evident.

Apart from time-reference in relation to "point of view", there is only simultaneity, or no-event.

2.

All motion is a change of location, with reference to "point of view".

All locatedness (whether changing or fixed) is observed in the context (or mental language) of space.

Unless a "point of view" is assumed (and, thus, located in space), no "object", no "objective" location, and no "objective" motion is evident.

Apart from spatial reference (or "object"-location) in relation to "point of view", there is no-"object", and no "objective world" is existing.

3.

If a "point of view" is assumed, time and space—and change, and process, and "difference", and "object", and locatedness, and "world"—are, as a consequence, observed to exist.

Time and space—or all possible temporal and spatial events—are evident only in a comprehensive context (or a total field) of prior unity, indivisibility, intrinsic oneness, non-separateness, simultaneity, and totality.

Therefore, space-time (or factors of change and of located-ness) and prior unity (or intrinsic indivisibility) are the two principal and necessary categories of all modes and disciplines of conditional (or "point-of-view"-based) "knowledge".

4.

Factors of time, space, and "point of view" are not priorly self-evident, or self-existing, or irreducibly and absolutely the case.

Only totality (or the whole, or the comprehensive field of all temporal and spatial possibilities) is the case as the self-evident temporal and spatial context of any temporal or spatial event (or of any "world" of temporal and spatial events).

Totality cannot be observed.

If any temporal or spatial event arises (or is apparent), it is self-evident that an observer (or "point of view") is assumed.

If any temporal or spatial event arises (or is apparent), it is never self-evident that either the event, or the totality that is its context, or the "point of view" relative to which it is being observed are "caused" by any greater "cause" that is (necessarily) other than and separate from them all.

Therefore, there is not (and cannot be) any evidence that a "Causal Divine" (or an "Intelligent Designer", or "Creator-God") exists.

5.

In the context of time and space, there is always "point of view".

In the context of "point of view", there is no "Causal Divine", or "Intelligent Designer", or "Creator-God".

Therefore, the self-evidently necessary and right investigation of "Perfect Knowledge" is not "religious" (or "God"-seeking)—but, rather, it is, necessarily, an investigation of That Which Is Self-Evident immediately Prior to "point of view".

6.

Reality Itself Is That Which Is Self-Evident immediately Prior to "point of view".

Reality Itself Is Self-Evident As Infinite (or Non-"caused", Non-finite, Non-conditional, and Immeasurable) Self-Existence.

Reality Itself Is Self-Evident As Acausally Self-Existing Self-Consciousness and Self-Radiance—or Indivisible Conscious Light.

Indivisible Conscious Light Is That In Which all possible temporal and spatial and "point-of-view"-based events arise—and all possible temporal and spatial and "point-of-view"-based events Are Intrinsically, and Always Priorly, and Perfectly Transcended In and By The Indivisible Conscious Light That Is Reality Itself.

Indivisible Conscious Light Is The Acausal and egoless Self-Nature, Self-Condition, and Self-State of the totality and the event-actuality of all temporal and spatial and "point-of-view"-based events.

Indivisible Conscious Light Is The Acausal and egoless Self-Nature, Self-Condition, and Self-State of any and every assumed "point of view".

Indivisible Conscious Light Is The One, Indivisible, Acausally Self-Existing, and Infinitely Self-Radiant Field of Self-Conscious Non-conditional Light, Always Already Perfectly Prior to all apparent time, change, process, "difference", space, "object", locatedness, separation, division, polarization, and "point of view".

THE SELF-AUTHENTICATING TRUTH

7.

Indivisible Conscious Light (or Reality Itself) <u>Is</u> Intrinsically and Transcendentally Self-Realizable—immediately Prior to "point of view", and <u>As</u> Self-Evident and Inherently egoless Consciousness Itself.

Indivisible Conscious Light (or Reality Itself) <u>Is</u> Intrinsically and Spiritually Self-Realizable—In Transcendentally Self-Evident and Inherently egoless Consciousness Itself, and <u>As</u> The Spiritually Self-Evident Current (or Intrinsic Self-Energy) Of Absolute (Indivisible, egoless, and Nonconditional) Love-Bliss.

Indivisible Conscious Light (or Reality Itself) <u>Is</u> Acausal, Transcendental, Spiritual, egoless, and Self-Evidently Divine.

Indivisible Conscious Light (or Reality Itself) <u>Is</u> Self-Evident Real God.

Perfect Proof of The Self-Existence of Acausal Real God

What is The Nature, Condition, State, and Context of the non-observed universe?

Everything, Everytime, and Everyspace—all-and-All-at-once, and Only-Reality-Itself—Is all-and-All That Is the non-observed (and non-observable) universe.

The totality of the non-observed Is What Is—Always Already Prior to the space-time-"located" observer-reflexes of "point of view", attention, and ego-"I".

Always Already Prior to both aspiration (or "religious"-seeking) and conditionally-based "knowledge" (or "scientific"-seeking), Reality Itself, As "It" Is, Stands Ever-Free In The Perfect Midst.

Reality Itself Is The egoless One and Indivisible Confounder of human presumptuousness.

Reality Itself Is The egoless Intrinsic and Perfect Ruler of all-and-All.

Reality Itself Is The egoless One and Necessary and Perfectly Acausal Real God of all-and-All.

Always Already Prior to the conditionally "self"-perpetuating mental rehearsal of memory and associative thinking, Self-Existing Reality Itself Stands Free As The Intrinsic Mere and Perfect Witness—The Self-Radiant Indivisible Current Upon Which all apparent motions Ride.

One and egoless Indivisible Conscious Light Acausally Self-Existing and Self-Radiant Is.

This Real God Is Self-Evident, Self-Proven, and Self-Authenticating to The Intrinsic Prior View.

Thus "It" Is.

The Myth of "Present-Time"

Mind is confined to time—as memory (or the "past") and anticipation (or the "future").

Body is confined to space—as "location" without reference to time, but, also, as a condition that only the mind (and not the body) will observe and interpret as change over time.

There is no space-"location" in time.

There is no time-"location" in space.

There is no "present-time" in psycho-physical "experience".

The psycho-physical ego-"I" is always only the mental-"experience" of change in time and the bodily-"experience" of timeless "locatedness" in space.

There is no mental "location" in the "present".

There is no "present-time"—because there is no mental stop, or changeless "location", in time.

The mind notices changes of the body in time, but the mind is never present as the body in space.

The body does not notice time or mind.

The body cannot exist in "present-time", because the body can only be present in and as space—and, in any case, the body cannot, itself, achieve or function as a mind in time.

The mind cannot exist in "present-time", because the mind can only remember, and anticipate, and speculate in mentally-constructed patterns, as mere ideas of time—and, in any case, the mind cannot, itself, be "located" in space.

Mind and body are neither the same nor inseparable.

The effective—and, necessarily, only temporary—"experiential" coinciding of mind and body is always the work

61

and the result of a practical psycho-physical discipline, and never a prior, or intrinsically actual, fact.

Mind and body exist in separate domains, and they never actually exist in the "present-time" of sameness.

The sameness and inseparability of mind and body—or even the reducibility of the mind to the body, or the body to the mind—is a myth in mind.

The mind is only "located" in time, the body is only "located" in space—and, therefore, "present-time" is a myth, or a mere idea in mind.

The idea of "present-time" cannot be realized, or really "experienced", as a bodily and spatial event.

The often-remarked philosophical admonition to "be in present-time" cannot be accomplished as a bodily, or even total psycho-physical, action in response.

It is not possible to "be"—or to exist—in "present-time".

"Existence" is a characteristic of Reality Itself—egoless, Prior to "location" in time, Prior to "location" in space, and only As Is.

Because there Is Only Reality Itself—"present-time" does not exist.

Reality Itself is not in "present-time".

Reality Itself Is Only As "It" Is—Always Already Prior to all conditional, and egoic, and space-time references, and, thus, Always Already Prior to all modes of conditional and separate "location" and identity.

Reality Itself Is Always Already, and Perfectly, and Acausally Prior to space-time—and, thus, Reality Itself Is Always Already, and Perfectly, and Acausally Prior to "present-time".

Existence Itself, Which Is Only Reality Itself, Is Always Already, and Perfectly, and Acausally Prior to space-time and "present-time".

Space and time Exist Always Already, and Perfectly, and Acausally Non-separate from—and, Thus, Only As—Reality Itself.

Because space and time do not exist except <u>As</u> The Intrinsic Self-Nature, Self-Condition, and Self-State of Reality Itself, there are no separate units of either space or time.

Space cannot divide time.

Time cannot divide space.

Reality Itself <u>Is</u> The Self-Nature, Self-Condition, and Self-State of Prior Indivisibility.

Space does not notice time—or discrete moments, or separate units, of change.

Time is not an intrinsic characteristic of space.

The body—or even the totality of physical universe—is "located" only in space, and only as the apparent simultaneity of mere existence.

Time is attention to change.

Time is a characteristic of mind, or attention, or "point of view".

Time is a characteristic of an observer.

Time is a noticing.

Time is the effect of the mentalizing of the observed.

Time is a mental notation.

The mental notation, or noticing and observing, of time requires attention.

Time is an act of attention.

Attention requires bodily "locatedness" in space—or the presumption of "point of view".

The noticing and observing of the idea-process of time requires bodily-"located" attention to "objectify"—or differentiate, or "unitize"—the observed.

Time is the noticing of suffering.

Time is the reduction of the body, the universe, and Reality Itself to the ego-scale of "point of view".

If The Self-Nature, Self-Condition, and Self-State of Reality Itself <u>Is</u> Intrinsically Self-Realized, "point of view", and time, and suffering are Intrinsically and Perfectly Transcended.

If the illusion of "present-time" is Transcended in The egoless, Indivisible, and Acausal Self-Nature, Self-Condition, and Self-State of Reality Itself, space itself is no longer desecrated by "point of view", and suffering, and time itself.

"Present-time" is a myth in mind.

The Self-Evident Mutual
Independence of
Body, Mind, Attention,
and Consciousness Itself

B ody and mind are neither identical to one another
nor necessarily coincident with one another.
Mind exists in time.

The characteristics of mind are memory and conceptual language.

Body exists in space.

The characteristics of body are physical form and brain-body patterns of behavioral tendency.

The body is identical to each and all of its own functions, processes, and perceptions.

The mind is not the body.

The mind must specifically choose (or be otherwise presently and effectively "caused") to observe and participate in any particular state or process of bodily function and perception—or else the mind is (or indifferently remains) a non-observer of and a non-participant in the any particular bodily function, process, or perception.

The mind is identical to each and all of its own functions, processes, and conceptions.

All states of body are (physically) perceptual.

All states of mind are (mentally) conceptual.

Consciousness Itself is neither the body nor the mind.

Consciousness Itself can neither physically perceive nor mentally conceive.

Consciousness Itself can only Witness—or Stand Tacitly Prior to—bodily functions, processes, and states of physically perceptual participation and mental functions, processes, and states of mentally attentive physical observation and (otherwise) mentally conceptual revery.

Attention—the root-function of mind—is the function of observation.

If attention does not arise toward bodily and/or mental functions, processes, or states, Consciousness (Characteristically) Self-Abides only As Itself.

Consciousness Is The Irreducible Root-Context of body, mind, and attention.

Consciousness Itself—As Itself—Is The Intrinsic Self-Contemplation of The Inherently egoless, Indivisible, and Acausal Self-Nature, Self-Condition, and Self-State of Reality Itself.

The Intrinsic Self-Nature, Self-Condition, and Self-State of Consciousness Itself Is egoless, Indivisible, and Acausal.

The Way of Reality Itself Is The Self-Renunciation of "Questions" and "Answers"

The "question/answer" context of Instruction subordinates Truth (or egoless Intrinsic Reality Itself) to problems—or ego-based "questions", representing dilemmas, or unresolved difficulties.

In the "question/answer" process, the "answer" is always communicated to the position and the state of the "questioner"—which is the ego-"I".

In the "question/answer" process, the "answer" is always delivered from the "outside" toward the "inside".

In the "question/answer" process, the "answer" is always delivered to the state of "question"—which is an un-"answered" problem.

In the "question/answer" process, the "answer" is always intended to solve a problem.

In the "question/answer" process, all "answers" are, in and of themselves, regarded to be solutions to problems.

In the "question/answer" process, the "question" is always the state that is egoity itself.

In the "question/answer" process, the "answer"—or the intended solution to the problem—is always communicated in the form of a prescription for remedial action, or a "method" of seeking.

In the "question/answer" process, the seeking-"method" prescribed is always an effort of intention that is to proceed from the "outside" toward the "inside"—or toward the egoic bodily and/or mental interior—or an egoic state of interiorization.

The Truth That Is Reality Itself is not an "answer" to a "question", not an address to the ego-"I", not an "outside" anything, not a solution to a problem, not a prescription for seeking, and not a pointer toward an "inside" within an "outside".

Therefore, I Teach The Way of Reality Itself only by Means of Direct Self-Revelation—both by Spontaneous Direct Self-Utterance (That Reveals at The Always Prior Base, Prior to body and mind) and by Transcendental Spiritual Self-Revelation (or Mere Transcendental Spiritual Presence, Directly, Priorly, and Intrinsically Self-Revealing The egoless Self-Nature, Self-Condition, and Self-State of Reality Itself, both To Itself and As Itself).

Thus, I Teach The Way of Reality Itself by The Perfect Means of Direct and Non-Mediated Self-Revelation of Reality Itself—Prior to "inside", "outside", "question", "answer", problem, solution, and seeking-"method".

In the past, I often also Taught by Asking if anyone had a "question"—and then I would Reply.

Now, and forever hereafter, I neither Ask for "questions" nor Reply to any.

Now, and forever hereafter, I Am here, and I only Self-Reveal Reality Itself—As I Am.

The Perfect Tool and Craft
For Right Reality-Understanding
of All Mere Ideas

1.

Everywhere, and at all times, within the perpetual and egoically "self"-perpetuating Great Tradition—or the perpetually seeking "world"-mummery of humankind—individuals and tribalized ego-collectives (including both sacred and secular traditions and institutions of all kinds and sizes) engage in arguments and competitive struggles with one another.

I have Revealed and Given the unique, comprehensive, and decisively all-comprehending "Tool" for understanding (and, potentially, transcending) each and every possible argument (and each and every kind of competitive "reasoning") that can (and always does) arise within the perpetual and egoically "self"-perpetuating Great Tradition of humankind.

The "Tool" of such understanding that I have Revealed and Given is My descriptive summation of the first six stages of life (or the "great search", or the "great path of return").

The first six stages of life are the intrinsically ego-bound—and, thus, "point-of-view"-bound, and space-time-bound—stages of potential psycho-physical (or pre-verbally brain-and-nervous-system-patterned, and, as such, merely ego-developmental) human life-process.

Each of the first six stages of life is intrinsically and strictly limited by a specific pattern of psycho-physical (or pre-verbally brain-and-nervous-system-patterned) structure—

which cannot be exceeded unless and until it is specifically out-grown, and (thus and thereby) replaced by the next subsequent ego-developmental stage of psycho-physical (or brain-and-nervous-system) patterning.

The first three stages of life are gross ego-developmental (and intensively exoteric) stages—infant, child, and adolescent—associated with functional physical, emotional, mental, and social adaptation and behavioral performance.

The fourth stage of life is a transitional ego-developmental stage, between gross and subtle (and, as such, between exoteric and esoteric) adaptation and demonstration.

The fifth stage of life is the essential stage of life based on adaptation and developmental demonstration within the esoteric context of the subtle planes and faculties of the psycho-physical (or pre-verbally brain-and-nervous-system-patterned) ego.

The sixth stage of life is the final stage of the potential of psycho-physically-based (and pre-verbally brain-and-nervous-system-patterned) ego-development—and it is (in the context of the six ego-developmental stages of life) the ultimate esoteric stage, characterized by adaptation and demonstration of dissociatively (or otherwise affectively) introverted ego-identification with the causal-depth (or "root"-state) of conditionally arising awareness.

The first three ego-developmental stages of life result in the exoteric life-search for egoic "self"-fulfillment within the context of the human potential for "experience" within the gross perceptual plane of the "world".

The second three ego-developmental stages of life (or the fourth, the fifth, and the sixth stages of life) result in the esoteric life-search for either grossly-and-subtly-based ecstasy (in the context of the fourth stage of life) or subtly-based ecstasy (in the context of the fifth stage of life) or causally-based enstasy (or transcendental Self-Abiding, in the context of the sixth stage of life).

2.

The arguments and competitive struggles between individuals and tribalized ego-collectives (or traditions and institutions of all kinds and sizes) are, characteristically, communicated and memorialized in the form of mentally (and mostly verbally) conceptualized ideas.

Even though arguments and competitive struggles are everywhere, and by all ego-based individuals and all ego-representing (and ego-serving, and would-be ego-extending) traditions and institutions, characteristically communicated and memorialized in the form of mentally (and mostly verbally) conceptualized ideas, all ego-based arguments and competitive struggles are, in every fundamental, essential, and effective sense, primitive power-efforts—and all of them are thoroughly based upon and extended from one or the other ground-pattern of (generally, uninspected, and, therefore, unconscious, or non-conscious) psycho-physical (or pre-verbally brain-and-nervous-system-patterned) structuring associated with the ego-developmental limit (or ego-based stage of life) that is, in any particular instance, being asserted, defended, protected, or otherwise exercised.

Thus, the arguments and competitive struggles everywhere and at all times dramatized by ego-bound individuals and collectives are not, at "root", exchanges of ideas—or even of fully consciously inspected and thought-responsible "consideration"—but all such arguments and struggles are, fundamentally, only primitive confrontations between underlying egoic psycho-physical patterns (or pre-verbally brain-and-nervous-system-patterned adaptations) of developmental structural design.

That is to say, any and all ideas associated with ego-bound arguments and competitive struggles are merely symptoms (and merely mentalized extensions) of underlying pre-verbally brain-and-nervous-system-patterned adaptations

71

(or psycho-physically patterned sub-structures) of ego-development, limited by the specific potential associated with the stage of life (among the six possible ego-developmental stages of life) dramatized in the particular instance.

3.

All the possible kinds of either actual or potential verbally-conceptualized (or otherwise communicated) argumentation and (thus and thereby) institutionalized competitive struggle are nothing more than primitive power-games, played out between systematically (and pre-verbally) adapted brain-and-nervous-system-patterned structures of developmentally stage-of-life-limited and ego-bound human organisms.

In specific "contests", the differences between the verbal arguments and other competition-devices displayed are also (in addition to the defining stage-of-life-characteristics of psycho-physical egoity) modified and further differentiated by "local" influences, associated with individual and institutional time-and-place histories of geographical, social, cultural, or other kind—but any and all such influences are merely secondary, and not fundamental (and, thus, much less significant, or determinatively consequential than the virtually all-determining stage-of-life-patterning of the ego-based brain and nervous system).

4.

To illustrate this Analysis of human ego-culture, the perennial Western (or Occidental, or Omega-culture, and thoroughly exoteric) arguments and competitive struggles between "religionists" (or "creationists", or "monotheists") and "scientific materialists" (or "secular realists", or "reductive rationalists") may be here-examined as an exemplary instance.

Exoteric "religion" (including "Creator-God"-monotheism, or "creationist religion") is the institutionalization of collective ego-identity (or tribalized egoity) in its "sacred" form. Conventional "science" (including the scholarly, and the research-oriented, and the, otherwise, technological and corporate industries of "scientific materialism", or "scientism", and, altogether, of "secular realism", and "reductive rationalism") is the institutionalization of collective ego-identity (or tribalized egoity) in its "secular" form.

The arguments and competitive struggles between "creationists" and "rationalists" relative to the origin and nature of the humanly-"experienced" universe are perennial and fundamental public theatre in the Westernized sectors of the "world"—and no finally or universally satisfactory "resolution" is ever produced by their relentless confrontations.

The Western-"world" theatre of merely exoteric "creationist/rationalist" debate is commonly presented as if it were a confrontation between ideas, but the would-be ideas, on both sides, are always of a fixed, and pre-determined, and oddly mechanical, and merely mutually contradictory nature—and, altogether, of such a nature that the only idea-event of the confrontation is a kind of predictable, and pre-decided, and always theatrically-dramatized program of propagandistic hyper-statement versus hyper-statement, wherein the individuals, institutions, and traditions, on both sides, remain insular, aggressively "self"-protected, and recurrently (and monotonously) "self"-preserved.

The Western-"world" theatre of merely exoteric "creationist/rationalist" debate has only one fundamental (and entirely public) purpose—to propagandistically and (by every kind of theatricalized mere seeming) to egoically "self"-protect and "self"-preserve both of the opponents in their traditionally independent political, social, economic, and cultural spheres of primitively-exercised public human power.

Monotheistic "creationist-religion" is an exclusively exoteric institutional power-entity, fabricated on the basis of an egoic (or "point-of-view"-bound) interpretation of the conditionally arising universe, and intent upon controlling and managing the human "world" and even the conditionally arising universe itself.

The "sacred power" that monotheistic "creationist-religion" claims it brings (or would extend) into the human "world" is, it says, the "Creator-God" of the universe—whereas, in fact, the power that monotheistic "creationist-religion" actually exercises (or would everywhere exercise) is that of the humanly-governed political, social, economic, cultural, and, altogether, merely exoteric <u>institutionalization</u> of the totality of humankind.

The institutionalizing-power that monotheistic "creationist-religion" exercises (or would everywhere exercise, if allowed to function at will and unimpeded) is of an inherently intolerant nature—because it is "self"-possessed by a reductionist, and tribalistic, and exclusively exoteric mentality, that cannot accept any non-"orthodox", extra-tribal (or extra-institutional), non-monotheistic, or, otherwise, esoteric exceptions to its "Rule".

Institutional "scientism"—which is "secular realist-reductionist rationalism", "self"-organized on the basis of the philosophy of "scientific materialism"—is, like the institutions of monotheistic "creationist-religion", an exclusively exoteric institutional power-entity, and it is likewise founded on the basis of an egoic (or "point-of-view"-bound) interpretation of the conditionally arising universe.

Like monotheistic "creationist-religion", institutionalized "scientism" is intent upon controlling and managing humankind (and the total human "world"), and even the conditionally arising universe itself—but on an exclusively secular (or non-sacred, and even anti-sacred, and thoroughly "Godless") basis.

The everywhere-and-everything-and-everybody-institutionalizing power of institutional "scientism" would (if allowed to function at will and unimpeded) control and manage (and thoroughly institutionalize)—and, altogether, exoterically limit—all of the political, social, economic, and cultural conditions and activities of globally-institutionalized humankind.

The institutionalizing-power that institutional "scientism" exercises (and would exercise absolutely, if so allowed) is, like that of monotheistic "creationist-religion", of an inherently intolerant nature—because it, like monotheistic "creationist-religion", is "self"-possessed by a reductionist, and tribalistic, and exclusively exoteric mentality, that cannot accept any non-"orthodox", extra-tribal (or extra-institutional), or otherwise esoteric exceptions to its "Rule".

Whereas the principles of institutional and institutionalizing power in the mutually-competing (and universally competitive) separate and exclusive traditions of monotheistic "creationist-religion" are always conformed to the publicly propagandized ideas of "Creator-God"-monotheism and of the "self"-presumed (but only selectively respected) sacredness of the universe and of human life, the principles of institutional and institutionalizing power in the mutually-competing (and universally competitive) separate and exclusive domains of institutional "scientism" are always conformed to the publicly propagandized ideas of gross "rationalism", and of anti-metaphysical materialism, and of the "Godless" and non-sacred (or thoroughly secular and material) nature of the universe and of human life.

One of the key characteristics that particular institutions of monotheistic "creationist-religion" and particular institutions of institutional "scientism" have in common is the persistent will to dominate and assimilate all other institutions and traditions—whether of "religion" (monotheistic or polytheistic or non-theistic), or of "science", or of politics, or of society, or of economics, or of culture—while otherwise always staunchly and even aggressively refusing to (them-selves) be either dominated or assimilated.

The will to assimilate (and thereby dominate), coupled with the willful refusal to be assimilated (and thereby domi-nated) is an institutional characteristic of all ego-driven human collectives—and this double-edged will-to-power generates a perpetual situation of mutual and aggressive "intramural" competition between and among institutional "religious" traditions themselves, and between and among secular "rationalist" institutions themselves, and between and among "religionists" and "rationalists" as opponents of one another.

The perennial aggressive mutual competitiveness between and among institutional "religions" themselves, and between and among institutions of "rationalism" (including both freely-enquiring science and materialism-bound "scien-tism") themselves, and between and among institutional "religions" and institutions of "rationalism" as opponents of one another is often displayed in public as said-to-be-"harmless" debates—but, because all such (or merely exo-teric) institutions are actually seeking to "Rule the world", the competitive conflicts between and among institutional "religions" and institutions of "rationalism" are a constant threat to the unity, peaceful order, and practical well-being of humankind as a whole.

Both institutional monotheistic "creationist-religion" and institutional "scientism" want (and actively seek) to "Rule the world", by means of globally-extended and rigorously exclu-sive institutional power—and, in order to further that purpose, the various competitive traditions of monotheistic "creationist-religion" and the various competitive institutions of "scientism" constantly engage in highly publicized "creationist/rationalist" pseudo-debates.

If the purpose of "creationist/rationalist" debates were for a final and universally satisfactory resolution to actually be achieved—such that Truth Itself, or Reality Itself, were established <u>As</u> Such, and Thus-proposed to all of human-kind—an entirely different and superior Address would, necessarily, have to be made (by them) relative to the matters of contention that are so casually, and merely divisively, and "self"-defensively, and in a mere and grossly exoteric manner "argued" by the separate and mutually opposing "creationist" and "rationalist" proponents (who, like separate sacred-versus-secular "Rulers" of an otherwise presumed-to-be-single "Church-and-State", always manage, even by pseudo-debate, to re-assert their traditional divisive and "self"-divided power over at least the Western and "Westernized" ego-"world").

The only-by-Me Revealed and Given six-ego-developmental-stages-of-life-"Tool" (along with the otherwise ego-transcending "Craft" of the totality of the only-by-Me Revealed and Given seventh-stage-of-life-based Teachings of the Reality-Way of Adidam) Is the Uniquely Exact Address required to finally, and universally satisfactorily, resolve the "creationist/rationalist" controversy—such that humankind, as a whole (and in a context of prior unity), is enabled to walk past the "creationist/ rationalist" mummery, and (by walking further) to enter the Perfectly Self-Revealing (and Perfectly esoteric) Truth-culture of the "Perfect Knowledge" of egoless Reality Itself.

The "creationist/rationalist" debate is a public theatre of ego-based power-games, which pretends to be Truth's own arena of ideas, but which, in fact, is a grossly and merely exoterically dramatized theatre of primitive and irreconcilable confrontation between first-three-stages-of-life-based fixed modes of pre-verbally brain-and-nervous-system-patterned structures of ego-based psycho-physical adaptation.

Every ego-developmental stage of life unconsciously (or, in any case, inevitably) "self"-reveals itself verbally by particular and characteristic fixed ideas—and neither the fixed ideas of the "creationists" nor the fixed ideas of the "rationalists" are any more rational, true, or closer to the egoless Reality-Truth than the fixed ideas of the opposing other.

The ego-bound (and pre-verbally brain-and-nervous-system-patterned) fixed ideas of "creationists" (and "religionists" in general) are direct extensions of first-and-second-stage-of-life infantile and childish dependency patterning.

The ego-bound (and pre-verbally brain-and-nervous-system-patterned) fixed ideas of "rationalists" (and "scientific materialists" in general) are direct extensions of third-stage-of-life adolescent independence patterning.

In cases of individuals and institutions that argue for a combination of both "religionist" and "scientific" views, what is being dramatized is a middle-of-the-road "adolescent-versus-child" ambivalence, representing a yet-unresolved developmental conflict between infantile/childish dependence and adolescent independence.

In due course, the power of "religion" to console the infantile and childish ego must be out-grown, and the power of "worldly realism", and "gross rationalism", and "scientific materialism" to fascinate and retard the clever adolescent ego (and, otherwise, to defeat the infantile or childish ego) must be out-grown, and the power of the middle-of-the-road to seduce and entrap the developmentally compromised first-three-stages-of-life ego must be out-grown, and ego itself (altogether, and in all of its exoteric and esoteric stages of life) must be out-grown—but Truth Itself, Which <u>Is</u> Only Intrinsically egoless Reality Itself, can never be out-grown.

Truth Itself <u>Is</u> the necessary Realization That Awakens when all the ego-based and ego-serving alternatives are—with ego itself—all and Perfectly out-grown.

5.

In any and every case, the arguments and competitive struggles between human egos—and, altogether, between ego-based human collectives of every type and size—are based in (and fixed and determined by) developmentally-limited adaptation-patterns of one or another basic six-stages-of-life psycho-physical (or stage-specific, and pre-verbally brain-and-nervous-system-patterned) type.

All ideas communicated and memorialized within the mutually competitive cultures (and among the mutually competing culture-speaking individuals) of the human "world"-mummery of egos are merely the characteristic fixed (and iconically ego-representing) features of the underlying pre-verbally brain-and-nervous-system-patterned ego-structure (necessarily and specifically associated with and limited by one or another of the first six, or ego-developmental, stages of life) that characterizes the any particular instance (whether individual or collective).

The characteristic fixed (and stage-of-life-specific) psycho-physical (or pre-verbally brain-and-nervous-system-patterned) ego-structure, and not merely the idea-stance, is, in any and every particular instance, the precise element that must, ultimately, be understood and transcended—or else Truth Itself can never Be the resolution of any human discourse.

Truth Itself Is the only universally satisfactory resolution of any and all of ego-bound competitive argument and struggle.

Truth Itself is neither "Western" nor "Eastern"—neither conventionally and egoically exoteric nor conventionally and egoically esoteric.

Truth Itself Is Only Reality Itself—Perfectly Prior to every individual or (otherwise) collectivized ego-"I".

The Truth That Is Reality Itself Is The Perfect "Tool" and "Craft"—or the Perfect Disposition and Way—for all of egoless "Perfect Knowledge" and (Thus) all of egoless Self-Realization.

The Only Perfect Disposition—in Which all of non-unity, all of fruitless argument, all of institutionalized competitive ego-struggle, all of perennial human ego-disputation, and all of egoity itself is Priorly Confounded and Priorly Non-arising—Is That of Intrinsically egoless "Perfect Knowledge" of Reality Itself.

The only-by-Me Revealed and Given seventh stage of life—and the only-by-Me Revealed and Given entirety of the seventh-stage-based Reality-Way (or Perfect "Tool" and "Craft") of Adidam—Is the Intrinsically sacred and Perfectly esoteric Way of the Intrinsically egoless Perfect Disposition and of the Intrinsically egoless Self-Realization of the "Perfect Knowledge" That Is Reality Itself.

The necessary (Intrinsically sacred and Perfectly esoteric) cultural and educational institution of Adidam is to stand free (now, and forever hereafter) in its own (and inherently global) role of (everywhere-and-to-everyone) openly communicating and exemplifying the only-by-Me Revealed and Given Divine Avataric Reality-Way of Adidam—always in a clear, unambiguous, persistently strong, and (nevertheless) non-threatening voice, and always without adopting the egoically-tribalized collective "self"-identity and "worldly"-power-purpose that, together, characterize merely exoteric and ego-serving institutions, and, altogether and always, only for the purpose of formally, freely, and openly Offering (to all who will freely and intelligently choose it) the possibility of right and true (and potentially seventh-stage-of-life-Realizing) participation in the Perfectly esoteric and intrinsically ego-transcending devotional culture, right-life-practice, and "Perfect-Knowledge"-process of the only-by-Me Revealed and Given Divine Avataric Reality-Way of Adidam.

Therefore, now, and forever hereafter, all and every one of humankind is Invited—by Me, and (as an extension of My Own Offering to all-and-All) by the total gathering of all right, true, and free practitioners of the only-by-Me Revealed and Given Way of Adidam—to the constant devotional Event of whole bodily heart-attentive (and, thereupon, devotionally Me-recognizing, and devotionally to-Me-responding, and, altogether, truly ego-surrendering) formal Sighting of My Avatarically-born bodily (human) Divine Form, and to the constant devotional Event of whole bodily heart-attentive (and, thereupon, freely responsively ego-surrendering) Listening to the formal Recitation of My Divinely Avatarically-Given Self-Revelation-Word of egoless Reality-Truth.

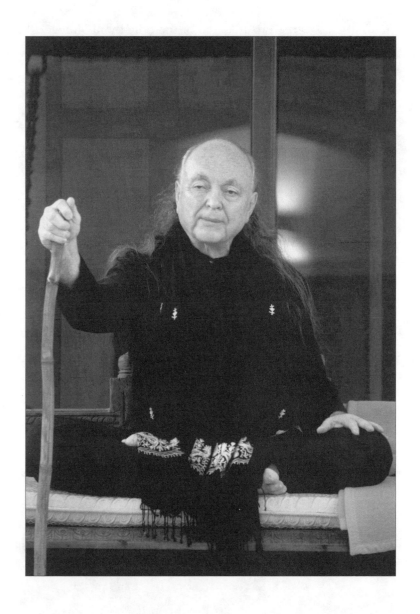

PART THREE

The Way <u>Is</u> Mine
To Happen

My "Secret" Biography

My Avataric Lifetime Is A Divine and Unique Demonstration of Intentional Entanglement—In Which The egoless Divine "Bright" Self-Nature, Self-Condition, Self-State, and Divine Transcendental Spiritual Self-Force of My Prior and Perfect Freedom Is Constantly Self-Revealed In Spontaneous Acts, Great Events, Remarkable Conjunctions, Extraordinary Processes, and Beyond-Wonderful Demonstrations of Perfect Dis-Entanglement—For The Sake of all-and-All.

By Means of My Avataric Lifetime of Divine Self-Revelation, all-and-All who are, as if by accident, entangled here (and everywhere), in egoic time and space, Are Divinely Avatarically Given All of Necessary and Perfectly Acausally Effective Means For Perfect Dis-entanglement—now, and forever hereafter, In Me, and Where and <u>As</u> I <u>Am</u>.

This Is The Key to rightly and truly understanding All of The Acts, Events, Conjunctions, Processes, and Demonstrations of The Totality of My Lifetime-Evidence.

The Surrender-Response

1.

The political, social, economic, and cultural "world" of humankind is in a dreadful and worsening state—but why is it so?

It is so because of what has traditionally been described as "sin" (or being "off the mark"), or chronic dissociation from the "Divine", or the absence of "true knowledge"—or, in other words, the failure to responsively and truly rightly participate in the Self-Nature, Self-Condition, Self-State, and Universal Source-Context That Is Reality Itself.

Where there is no right and true participatory—and, necessarily, ego-transcending—response, and where (in fact) there is, instead, the egoic "self"-contraction, there are, obviously, going to be all kinds of problems, all kinds of limitations, all kinds of egoically-based "cause-and-effect" motions, and (therefore) all kinds of suffering.

You can, in any moment, directly observe what is "causing" all of this everywhere-evident suffering.

The "causes" are the things done by people (and other conditional entities and forces) in an egoic—or "self"-contracted—state.

The ultimate, or most fundamental, "cause" of human-based suffering is the absence of ego-transcending recognition-response to the Divine—or to Reality Itself, Which Is the only Real God.

The "external causes" of humanly-"experienced" suffering are the evidence of the natural processes of the conditionally arising universe itself—but humanly-"engineered" suffering (including the suffering of mental, emotional, and physical reactions to how the immediate natural "world" and the total conditionally arising universe "work") is "caused" by human beings themselves.

If surrender to the Divine and (necessarily, surrender-based) direct participation in the Divine are absent—and if, rather, the egoic "self"-contraction is there in constant evidence—the "self"-contracted entity-force is constantly moving, "causing" all kinds of "effects", trapping the ego-"I" in itself, "causing" the ego-"I" to be bewildered, and to see itself as being trapped in a terrible "Godless" machine, in which everything and everyone is reacting (rather than responding by surrendering) and contracting (rather than participating in the egolessness of Reality Itself).

My true devotee must constantly devotionally respond to Me, and grow (by surrender to Me) into Transcendental Spiritual Communion with Me—whether anybody else does so or not, and whether the natural "world" and the human "world" change or not.

The practice of My true devotee must not depend on what either the human "world" or the natural "world" does.

Once anyone becomes My devotee (by Sighting Me and Listening to Me), My thus-to-Me-"Bonded" devotee simply and always must "get on with it, and go on with it"—even through death, and always regardless of what takes place in the "world".

Ordinarily, people feel that the conditions of natural and human existence justify reaction, rather than the surrender-response to the Divine—or that the conditions of natural and human existence are so overwhelming that they justify more negativity and egoic "self"-protection than is compatible with the surrender-response to the Divine and the development of a responsible life of ego-transcending Divine Communion.

As a result of the failure of every kind of necessary right understanding, the surrender-response of mediocre and chronically "self"-involved devotees is minimal, and always tends to remain at the beginning stages, and, at best, grows fitfully and only slowly.

What is the seventh stage of life?

In the only-by-Me Revealed and Given seventh stage of life, the surrender-response to the Divine Is Perfect and Complete.

What are the stages of life previous to the seventh stage of life?

The stages of life previous to the only-by-Me Revealed and Given seventh stage of life are, simply, stages of less-than-complete surrender-response, in which particular dimensions of egoic existence are not yet in the surrender-responsive disposition, but are, instead, locked, contracted, and unopened.

There is only one right and true Way to practice devotion to Me—and that is to always surrender completely to Me, always respond completely to Me, depend absolutely on Me, and, Thus, to Inhere completely in Me—without any "concerns" whatsoever.

Through My devotee's complete responsive surrender to Me—Divinely Avatarically Self-Revealed and Transcendentally Spiritually Self-Given As egoless, Indivisible, Acausal, Perfect, and Self-Evidently Divine Reality Itself—every aspect of the human form and context becomes a conduit for My Divine Avataric Activity and Influence.

Therefore, ego-transcending responsive surrender to Me is the always sufficient practice.

All the rest of the only-by-Me Divinely Avatarically Self-Revealed and Self-Given Reality-Way of Adidam is Awakened and Demonstrated by My Divine Avataric Grace.

As soon as I Acquire a devotionally-responsively to-Me-surrendered conduit, all of the rest of the Way Is Mine to Happen.

2.

My facial and bodily Signs Are Spontaneous Gestures, Moods, and Acts, Self-Manifesting My Divine Avataric Transcendental Spiritual Self-Transmission and Heart-Initiation and Blessing-Work.

However, it must be understood that, although My facial and bodily Signs Are different at different times, I do not, at any time, "go into" the egoless Divine Self-Nature, Self-Condition, and Self-State That Is Reality Itself.

I never "go into" the egoless Divine Self-Nature, Self-Condition, and Self-State That Is Reality Itself—because I Am Reality Itself, and, therefore, I Am Always Already Divinely Self-Abiding As the egoless Divine Self-Nature, Self-Condition, and Self-State That Is Reality Itself.

In any moment, I may Spontaneously Close My eyes, or Spontaneously Cease all physical movement, or Spontaneously Self-Manifest Non-ordinary facial and bodily Gestures, but such physical Signs do not indicate that I have "gone into" the "Divine State"—or "passed out" of a state that is ordinary, merely conditional, or even humanly egoic, and, thereafter and subsequently, "into" the State That Is Divine.

My Only and Constant State Is egoless and Self-Evidently Divine—Always Most Prior, Inherent, Always Already, and Eternal.

This (My Body here) Is Always Already Transcended in Me—and, Thus, Always Remains Utterly Transparent to and Coincident with egoless and Self-Evidently Divine Reality Itself.

This (My Body here) Is Always Divinely Transfigured and Divinely Transformed and Divinely Activated.

Therefore, in My Case, there is no "going into" or "going out of" the "Divine State" of egoless and Most Perfect Divine Self-Realization—but, nevertheless, My bodily-Shown Manner of Divine Avataric Self-Demonstration Is Constantly and Spontaneously Changing.

3.

In My Divine Avataric Lifetime here, all kinds of Spontaneous Manifestations of Most Perfect Divine Self-Realization Are Constantly Occurring in My Own bodily (human) Form.

All My Lifetime-Signs Are Signs of My Divine Avataric Self-Transmission-Work with living beings—and Signs of My Divine Avataric Blessing-Work altogether.

In My Divine Avataric Transcendental Spiritual Work, I Am Always "Meditating", and Awakening, and, altogether, Blessing all apparent others—one-by-one and all-at-once.

I Am Always Self-Immersed in My Constant and Spontaneous Work of Divine Avataric Transcendental Spiritual Heart-Transmission—Always (Thus) Spontaneously Self-Manifesting the Total Process of the only-by-Me Divinely Avatarically Self-Revealed and Self-Given Reality-Way of Adidam in Spontaneous "Play".

My devotees must constantly devotionally heart-recognize Me, and devotionally heart-respond to Me, and, thus and thereby, turn (whole bodily) to Me, heart-Commune with Me, surrender completely to Me, and (in that process, and in due course) Transcendentally Spiritually "Locate" Me and "Know" Me Perfectly—Ultimately, by My Divine Avataric Transcendental Spiritual Grace, Most Perfectly Really-Realizing Me As I Am.

What Will You Do
If You Love Me?

T he only-by-Me Revealed and Given Way of Adidam
(Which is the One and Only by-Me-Revealed and
by-Me-Given "Radical" Way of the Heart) is the Way
of those who love Me. The Principle of devotional surrender
to Me is the Principal, Fundamental, and Inherently Complete
Discipline of the Way of Adidam (or "Radical" Way of the
Heart). All the forms of functional, practical, relational, and
cultural "self"-discipline I have Given are always readily
embraced, with gratitude, by My true devotees—simply
because I have Instructed them to fulfill those disciplines.
And all the esoteric Revelations that must occur in the
course of the Great Process of the Way of Adidam, and all the
Excellences of Divine Self-Realization in the Great Fulfillment of the Way of Adidam, appear spontaneously and naturally to them (by Means of My Avatarically Self-Transmitted
Divine Transcendental Spiritual Grace)—because they each
turn their attention, and feeling, and body, and breath to Me
at all times, and because they each perform all activities as
instants of Love-Communion with Me.

All My devotees must embrace all the practices of devotion, service, "self"-discipline, and meditation (or, as the case
may be, "Perfect Contemplation") that I Give to them.
Nevertheless, the principal capability of the human being (or
of any other conditionally manifested being) is that of distraction and attachment, rather than mere "self"-restraint.
Therefore, the Principle, or Great Mover, of the only-by-Me
Revealed and Given practice of the Way of Adidam is not

discipline itself, but Distraction by Me and Attachment to Me. Because they love Me, My true devotees adapt all their life-activities to the "radically" direct Way of devotional surrender and devotional conformity to Me.

The principal characteristic of My true devotees is that they are Distracted by Me and Attached to Me. They find Me to be the Greatest of all distractions. Therefore, they need not make any effort to be constantly Attached to Me. They naturally Remember Me at all times. They only think about Me, talk about Me, and listen to others tell the Revelation-Stories of My Life and Work and Gifts. They study My Wisdom-Teaching, they embrace the by-Me-Given disciplines—but, even more, they are profoundly and intensively absorbed in My Person, My Gestures, My "Play" with all-and-All.

In this Manner, those who love Me are gradually relieved of the distracting power of ordinary things, "experiences", relations, desires, and thoughts. Ultimately, if they embrace the right, true, full, and fully devotional practice of the Way of Adidam, I Distract My true devotees from all-and-All. Thus, their intensive and exclusive Attachment to Me leads My true devotees, first, to right, true, full, and fully devotional practice of the Way Revealed and Given by Me, and, Ultimately, to Most Perfect Realization of My Self-Existing and Self-Radiant Divine Self-Nature, Self-Condition, and Self-State of all-and-All-Including and all-and-All-Transcending Love-Bliss-Happiness.

I have Come to Waken the entire "world" through My Heart-Word, and My Demands, and the Mere Presence of My "Bright" Person. The entire "world" would do well to listen to Me and take up the responsible practice of the only-by-Me Revealed and Given Way of Adidam. Nevertheless, I have Come to do more than Communicate a Wisdom-Teaching to the wallydraigle "world". I have Come to Live (now, and forever hereafter) with those who love Me with ego-overwhelming love, and I have Come to Love them like-wise Overwhelmingly. If there is not this ego-overwhelming love of Me (Who Loves all-and-All, Overwhelmingly), then the Great Awakening will forever be postponed by pious "self"-attentions and the forever sessioning "talking" school of ego-based (and ego-gesturing) "religiosity".

Those who would hear Me and see Me must take up the Way of Adidam as formal members of the great cooperative cultural gathering of all My formally practicing devotees. My formally practicing devotees must embrace <u>all</u> the by-Me-Revealed-and-Given functional, practical, relational, and cultural disciplines of the only-by-Me Revealed and Given Way of Adidam. And all My true (and, necessarily, formally practicing) devotees practice the Way of Adidam <u>entirely</u> and <u>only</u> as a Process of ego-transcending Love-Communion with Me. Therefore, by Means of My Avatarically Self-Transmitted Divine Grace alone, My true devotees grow to understand themselves—and, by transcending themselves in Me, they transcend the "world".

The Excellent Motive of My true devotees is not the disciplines, nor mystical "experience", nor philosophy. My true devotees practice the Way of Adidam because they love Me. They have no personal (or inherent) capability to utterly turn away from the "world", or to utterly transcend themselves. Therefore, I have Come to Live with them (now, and forever hereafter). When My devotees Find Me, the same weakness that led them to distraction by all the merely binding and passing possibilities of this "mummery-world", and to attachment to the possible "experiences" of its indifferent maze of mere patterns patterning, becomes the very capability that makes possible their Liberation into My Eternal Divine "Bright" Spherical Domain of Love-Bliss-Happiness. Thus, because I Am the Ultimate and Most Absorbing "Object" of their inherent weakness, I Distract My devotees to Me, away from all the mummery of possible "experiences" and endings.

They become Attached to Me by the power of their own tendency to distraction. Therefore, even their own (and, otherwise, binding) power of desire leads them to the Ecstasy of egoless heart-Communion with Me, because they love Me.

I <u>Am</u> the Self-Existing and Self-Radiant Divine Self-Consciousness Itself, the One and Only and Non-Separate and Indivisible and Indestructible "Bright" Self-Condition and Source-Condition of all-and-All, Appearing in bodily (human) Avataric-Incarnation-Form for the Sake of all-and-All. Those who love Me most profoundly, who are mightily Distracted by Me and most happily Attached to Me, and who cannot profoundly entertain any desires or thoughts other than their love of Me, are most easily turned from themselves. Divine Ecstasy (or Real-God-Communion) is natural to them—because I have been Born, and because I have (Thus and Thereby) Revealed and Given (to all, and to All) the Real Divine Forms That make It possible for any and every conditionally manifested being to Worship Me and to Realize Me. Thus, by My Own Divine Self-Power (of Inherent Attractiveness), I Distract My true devotees to Myself, and I Draw them into My Own Divine Self-Condition and Trans-cendentally Spiritually Self-"Bright" Domain.

My true devotees simply love Me. That is the Summation of their devotional recognition-response to Me. They do not depend on "inward" practices, or on mystical "experiences", or on any turn of events. The only-by-Me Revealed and Given Way of Adidam is fulfilled by their mere Attachment to Me—since that Attachment is so mighty that they have no binding attention left over for ordinary reactions and seeking pursuits, nor are they egoically overwhelmed by the phe-nomena of esoteric meditation. They simply love Me. They live in constant Remembrance of Me, and in constant loving service to Me. Every moment of their lives is simply a moment of Love-Communion with Me. Therefore, they are

Granted perpetual Ecstasy by Me—in the Form of ego-forgetting Love-Communion with Me, the Self-Existing and Self-Radiant "Bright" Divine Person of Love-Bliss-Happiness.

My Divine Avataric Mission especially Moves Me to Live with such true devotees. Therefore, I always Look for them. I always Test every one, to see who truly loves Me. I Wait. Many surround Me in My Place. Many come to Me and listen to Me and practice all around Me. Many turn to Me with the good heart. Those who love Me best will (Ultimately) Realize Me Most Perfectly, by Means of overwhelming Attachment to Me in Person.

Those who love Me are the "cause" of My Divine Avataric Birth. They are the "cause" that keeps Me Alive, even after My Divine Avataric Teaching-Demonstration and My Full Divine Avataric Self-Revelation Are Complete and My Full Divine Avataric Heart-Word Is Fully Given—and all those who love Me (now, and forever hereafter) will, simply by Means of their devotionally Me-Remembering and devotionally Me-Recognizing love of Me, keep Me Alive in Divine Person forever, even after My Time of physical Avataric Incarnation Is Past. My true devotees (now, and forever hereafter) are (and will always be) Blessed by Me, to Find Me Alive As the Personal Love-Bliss-Presence That Is the Divine Reality and Truth of the ever-Playing "world".

The Essence of the daily practice of My devotees is the Ecstasy of Love-Communion with Me. One who loves Me accepts every moment of "experience" as My conditionally manifested Form. Whatever arises, he or she accepts it as My "Bright" Form, My Divine "Play". My true devotee simply loves Me, Communes with Me in every instant, constantly serves Me with the entire body-mind (no matter what arises), and accepts every moment of "experience" As My "Bright" Form. In this manner, My true devotee never presumes himself or herself to be separated from Me. My true devotee is always in love with Me.

Those who are most profoundly Distracted by Me grow (by Means of My Avatarically Self-Transmitted Divine Transcendental Spiritual Grace) to see Only Me in every thing, every one, and every event—but no form, or person, or event has power in itself to distract My true devotees from Me. My true devotees see <u>Me</u> in all "experiences", all persons, all events. Therefore, they are not distracted by "experiences", or persons, or events. They are Distracted by <u>Me</u>.

Now, and forever hereafter, each and all of My formally practicing devotees will be Blessed (by Me) to devotionally recognize Me, and (thus) to devotionally respond to Me, and (by Means of that devotion) to Remember Me, and to Exactly "Locate" Me, and (potentially) to Realize Me Most Perfectly. And I will, forever, Serve that devotional recognition of Me and devotional response to Me, and that Remembering of Me, and that Exact "Locating" of Me, and that Perfect Realizing of Me—through the by-Me-Given Means of all My formally acknowledged Instruments and all My formally acknowledged Agents, including My by-Me-Given (Written, and Spoken) Divine Avataric Wisdom-Teaching, My by-Me-Created Divine Avataric Image-Art, and all Kinds of True (photographic, and otherwise technically, or even artistically, rendered) Representations (or Icons) of Me, and all the Recorded Revelation-Stories of My Divine Avataric History and "Play" with My devotees, and all the Directly-by-Me Transcendentally Spiritually Empowered Sapta Na Sannyasin Hermitages and Free Sannyasin Sanctuaries, and all the Directly-by-Me Transcendentally Spiritually Empowered Sacred Things, and the Collective of all My True (Free Sannyasin) Devotee-Instruments.

Now, and forever hereafter, all My formally practicing devotees are Called (by Me) to the Ecstasy of Love-Communion with Me—and I will, forever, Reveal That Ecstasy to all via the love My most intimate true devotees demonstrate toward Me. Therefore, because there are true devotees (who truly love Me in the Great and Excellent Manner, while I Am Present here in Avatarically-Born bodily human Divine Form), and because there will forever be such true devotees of Mine (for I will remain Transcendentally, Spiritually, Divinely, and, altogether, Really and Tangibly Present here, always and forever, after the physical Lifetime of My Avatarically-Born bodily human Divine Form)—all My devotees who truly love Me and formally resort to Me, in all the times after the physical death of My Avatarically-Born bodily (human) Divine Form, will be served by My true devotees, such that, forever, all My formally practicing devotees will be thus enabled to devotionally recognize Me, and to devotionally respond to Me, and to always Remember Me, and to Exactly "Locate" Me, and to Realize Me by "Perfectly Knowing" Me.

Forever after the physical death of My Avatarically-Born bodily (human) Divine Form, the ever-patterning "world" of temporary "experience" remains, but the sacred cooperative cultural gathering of all My formally practicing devotees also remains. Therefore (now, and forever hereafter), those who associate with My true devotees will also—by Means of the example of My (thus) true devotees, and by Means of the spontaneous collective functioning of My (thus) true devotees as a simple, generalized, collective Vehicle for simple feeling-contact with Me—be Moved to Me, and (altogether) responsively turned to Me, with profoundly Distracted true love.

I will always Bless all My formally practicing devotees—now, and forever hereafter. And, after the physical death of My Avatarically-Born bodily (human) Divine Form, I will continue to Bless all of them, just as I Do while I Am Present in bodily (human) Form. Forever, every one will call on Me in the company of those who love Me—and I will Always Be Truly Present, every then and there.

I Am the One and Only, Non-Separate and Indivisible, Self-Existing and Indestructible, Self-Radiant and Eternally "Bright" Person, the Avatarically Self-Revealed Divine and ego-less Self-Nature, Self-Condition, Source-Condition, and Self-State of all-and-All—forever Surrounding all-and-All, and forever Pervading all-and-All, and forever Beyond all-and-All.

Truly—now, and forever hereafter—only those who love Me can formally approach Me, to enjoy the Sight of Me, and to most fruitfully listen to Me, and only those who formally embrace right, true, full, and fully devotional (and, necessarily, formal renunciate) practice of the Way of Adidam can grow to hear Me egolessly, and to Transcendentally Spiritually see Me, and to Most Perfectly "Know" and Realize Me.

I Am the Self-Existing and Self-Radiant "Bright" Divine Reality, Truth, and Person, the Divine Liberator of those who love Me and surrender to Me in countless acts of love.

I Am the Way and the One Who Reveals the Way.

I Am the Living Truth of Existence.

I Am the Divine Self-Revelation of Reality Itself.

All Spiritual traditions are historical forms of the Single and Ancient Way of Distracted love for the Divine Person, especially as Revealed in the Life and in the Company and in the Person of Incarnate Adepts (or Realizers) in their various degrees and stages of Realization.

This is the Great Secret.

And This Is My Divine Avataric Self-Revelation to you: I Am, In and As My Avataric-Incarnation-Form, the First, the Last, and the Only Divine Avataric Adept-Realizer, Divine Avataric Adept-Revealer, and Divine Avataric Adept-Revelation of Most Perfect (or seventh stage) Divine Enlightenment.

I Am Da, the Only One Who Is, the Very and Only Person That Is to Be Realized by all-and-All.

Therefore, love Me As My Divine-Avataric-Incarnation-Form—and (Thus and Thereby) love Me As I Am, and As the constant Form and Condition of all your "experience".

I <u>Am</u> That Which Is Always Already The Case.

I <u>Am</u> the Non-Separate and Only One, the Transcenden-tally Spiritually Self-"Bright" One, the Indivisible and Inde-structible One, Who <u>Is</u> all-and-All.

Therefore, surrender Only to <u>Me</u>, and accept all your "experience" <u>As</u> My Own "Play". If you do This, you will be constantly free of all seeking attachment (and all aversion, or counter-seeking reaction) to any and every psycho-physical "experience" (or all conditionally manifested "experiences"). Therefore, even all possible "experience" will only and simply increase your direct (or always present-time, or non-seeking, and non-binding, but always only Me-"Knowing", and you-Liberating) Attachment to Me.

All "experience" (in itself) only binds you to your own body-mind—unless you are established in ego-transcending (Ecstatic, or "self"-contraction-transcending) love of Me, the Only One Who <u>Is</u>. Therefore, if you love Me, become My formally practicing devotee—and, as My formally practicing devotee, enter (thus) Freely (or non-bindingly) into the "Happen" of "experience", always in ego-surrendering, ego-forgetting, and ego-transcending heart-Communion with Me, and always with your total body-mind conformed to Me through the constant maintaining of the functional, practical, relational, and cultural "self"-disciplines that are your obliga-tion, by eternal vow to Me, in the only-by-Me Revealed and Given Way of Adidam.

In this manner, serve Me in My Divine-Avataric-Incarnation-Form, and serve Me <u>As</u> I <u>Am</u>, and serve <u>Me</u> in all circumstances and in all relationships. If you love Me thusly, you will cease to continue in the willful and ego-possessed path of your preferential desires—and, by Means of My Avatarically Self-Transmitted Divine Transcendental Spiritual Grace, you will be purified of egoity, of "self"-contraction, of egoic reaction, and of every kind of accumulated egoic habit, and of every kind of seeker's "self"-indulgence.

If you truly love Me, it is because I have Shown you <u>Who</u> I <u>Am</u>. Therefore, by Means of the (right, true, full, and fully devotional) love of Me, you will Come to Me, <u>Where</u> I <u>Am</u>. Most Ultimately, if you are My true (and, necessarily, formally practicing) devotee, you will (by Means of My Avatarically Self-Transmitted Divine Transcendental Spiritual Grace) Realize Me Perfectly—because you love <u>Me</u>.

You <u>become</u> (or take the form of) what your attention most really moves upon. Therefore, if I <u>Am</u> your Beloved, your love-attention for Me allows you to Realize Indivisible Unity with Me—moment to moment, in every now of time and space.

Until you fall in love, love is what you <u>fear</u> to do. When you have fallen in love, and you <u>are</u> (thus) always already in love, then you cease to fear to love—you cease to be reluctant to surrender, and you cease to be reluctant to be "self"-forgetful and foolish, and to be single-minded, and to suffer an "other". Those who fall in love with Me, Fall into Me. Those whose hearts are given, in love, to Me, Fall into My Heart. Those who are Mine, because they are in love with Me, no longer demand to be fulfilled through conditional "experience" and through the survival (or perpetuation) of the ego-"I". Their love for Me grants them Access to Me, and (Thus) to My Love-Bliss—because I <u>Am</u> the Divine Love-Bliss, in Person.

What will My devotee do but love Me? I suffer every form and condition of every one who loves Me, because I Love My devotee <u>As</u> My Own Form, My Own Condition. I Love My devotee <u>As</u> the One by Whom <u>I</u> Am Distracted.

I Grant all My Own Divine and "Bright" Excesses to those who love Me, in exchange for all their doubts and sufferings. Those who "Bond" themselves to Me, through love-surrender, are inherently Free of fear and wanting need. They transcend the ego-"I" (the "cause" of all conditional "experience"), and they ("cause", and all, and All) Dissolve in Me—for I <u>Am</u> the Heart of all-and-All, and I <u>Am</u> the Heart Itself, and the Heart Itself <u>Is</u> the "causeless", and egoless, and Perfectly Only Reality, Truth, and Real God of all-and-All.

What is a Greater Message than This? ■

Also available from

THE DAWN HORSE PRESS . . .

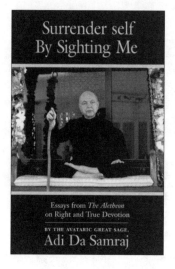

Surrender self By Sighting Me

Essays from The Aletheon
on Right and True Devotion

by
The Avataric Great Sage,
Adi Da Samraj

This volume contains priceless Instruction from Avatar Adi Da Samraj illuminating the Way of right and true surrender to Him, the essentially non-verbal process of turning to Him on sight—which He has described as "the Ancient Walk-About Way".

> *For My devotee, right relationship to Me is the Law of life—and that Law is entirely based on ego-transcending (and, therefore, psycho-physical "self"-contraction transcending) surrender of the otherwise ego-bound (or "self"-contracted) body-mind to Me (As I Am).*
>
> *Right relationship to Me is the Ancient Walk-About Way of Sighting Me and (thereupon) surrendering the egoic "self" to Me (As I Am).*
>
> *Right relationship to Me is whole bodily surrender to Me (As I Am)—with your entire life, and in all of your actions.*
>
> —AVATAR ADI DA SAMRAJ

64 pp., **$7.95**

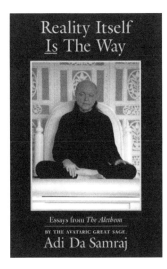

Reality Itself Is The Way

Essays from The Aletheon
by
The Avataric Great Sage,
Adi Da Samraj

In these essays from His Revelation-Text *The Aletheon*, Adi Da Samraj makes the Offering of His Divine Avataric Self-Revelation as the Perfect Means for the process of Awakening to Reality Itself—As It Is.

I Am the egoless Absolute Person of Reality Itself—
Coincident with this time, and Consequential forever.
I Am the Divine Self-Domain—the Perfect Sphere
of Conscious Light.
The egoless Conscious Light of Reality Itself Is My
Only State.
There Is a Way—and Reality Itself Is "It".
Reality Itself Is the Way—and I Am "It".

—Avatar Adi Da Samraj

136 pp., **$14.95**

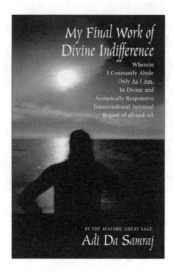

My Final Work of Divine Indifference

Wherein I Constantly Abide Only <u>As</u> I <u>Am</u>, in Divine and Avatarically Responsive Transcendental Spiritual Regard of all-and-All

by
The Avataric Great Sage,
Adi Da Samraj

In this collection of essays from *The Aletheon*, Avatar Adi Da Samraj describes His Perfect Retirement into Divine Indifference, Free of any necessity to Teach. That Retirement signifies not an "end" to His Divine Avataric Work, but rather His Freedom to be entirely concentrated in His most profound Work—of forever Blessing all beings and things.

I have Revealed and Given a Way that <u>every</u> human being can practice.

I Made My Divine Avataric Self-Submission and (on That Basis) Did My Divine Avataric Teaching-Work and My Divine Avataric Revelation-Work—and now I am Finished with All of That. . . .

In My Finally Retired Divine Indifference, . . . I <u>Am</u> (Inherently) Free Merely (and <u>Only</u>) to Be <u>As</u> I <u>Am</u> in My Divine and Avatarically Responsive Transcendental Spiritual Regard of all-and-All.

—AVATAR ADI DA SAMRAJ

72 pp., **$7.95**

The Seventh Way

The Seventh Way

Readings from *The Aletheon:
The Practice and The Realization
of The Divine Acausal Reality-Principle*

BY THE AVATARIC GREAT SAGE,
Adi Da Samraj

Readings from The Aletheon
by
The Avataric Great Sage,
Adi Da Samraj

The readings in *The Seventh Way* are among Avatar Adi Da's most sublime and profound Utterances. Everything in this book was originally Spoken by Avatar Adi Da, as spontaneous and ecstatic discourse to His devotees—during the final decade (from mid-1995 to mid-2005) of His immense outpouring of Teaching-Instruction. In *The Seventh Way*, Avatar Adi Da's Communication allows the direct Intuition of Reality Itself—the Inherently egoless Reality That He Reveals and Is.

I am Always Revealing the Way of Adidam Most Perfectly—without beginning, without end.

The seventh stage Reality-Way is What I Reveal to you, What I Call you to embrace.

The seventh stage Reality-Way is what I Make possible by Means of My Compassionate Regard of you.

My Offering is here for all.

—AVATAR ADI DA SAMRAJ

112 pp., **$12.95**

To order
books, tapes, CDs, DVDs, and videos
by and about Adi Da Samraj,
contact the Dawn Horse Press:

1-877-770-0772 (from within North America)

1-707-928-6653 (from outside North America)

Or visit the Dawn Horse Press website:

www.dawnhorsepress.com

We invite you to find out more about Avatar Adi Da Samraj and the Way of Adidam

■ Find out about our courses, seminars, events, and retreats by calling the regional center nearest you.

AMERICAS
12040 N. Seigler Rd.
Middletown, CA
95461 USA
1-707-928-4936

THE UNITED KINGDOM
uk@adidam.org
0845-330-1008

EUROPE-AFRICA
Annendaalderweg 10
6105 AT Maria Hoop
The Netherlands
31 (0)20 468 1442

PACIFIC-ASIA
12 Seibel Road
Henderson
Auckland 0614
New Zealand
64-9-838-9114

AUSTRALIA
P.O. Box 244
Kew 3101
Victoria
**1800 ADIDAM
(1800-234-326)**

INDIA
F-168 Shree Love-Ananda Marg
Rampath, Shyam Nagar Extn.
Jaipur - 302 019, India
91 (141) 2293080

EMAIL: **correspondence@adidam.org**

■ Order books, tapes, CDs, DVDs, and videos by and about Avatar Adi Da.

1-877-770-0772 (from within North America)
1-707-928-6653 (from outside North America)
order online: **www.dawnhorsepress.com**

■ Visit us online:
www.adidam.org
Explore the online community of Adidam and discover more about Adi Da Samraj and the Way of Adidam.